A B
THE S

By
HUGH CANTLIE

Over 200 pubs, hotels, restaurants and
places of interest which are about five
minutes from a Motorway junction

Published by Cheviot Books

1st Edition   September 2001
Reprint   January 2002
2nd Edition   October 2002

Copyright	Hugh Cantlie
Illustrations	Hugh Cantlie
Plans	Paul Cantlie
Maps	John Lee
Layout & Design	Tracy Coxon
Software consultant	Alistair MacDonald Smith

Printed and bound by Stephens & George Magazines

A catalogue record of this book is available from the British Library.

Please note
The author & publishers have made every effort to ensure the accuracy of the information in the book at the time of going to press. However, they cannot accept responsibility for any loss, injury or inconvenience resulting from the use of the information contained in this guide.

Cheviot Books, Belford Hall, Belford, Northumberland NE70 7EY or
E Mail: enquiries@cheviotbooks.co.uk
Website: www.cheviotbooks.com

CONTENTS

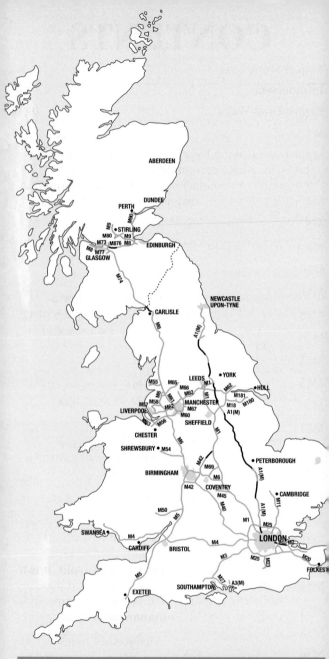

THE MOTORWAY NETWORK

Introduction

The Purpose of the Guide

Nearly every motorway junction seems to offer the possibility of getting away from the pressure of intensive driving for a short while for a meal or a break in calmer surroundings. It is only the uncertainty of whether such a haven exists or how long it will take to resume the journey that makes you reluctant to risk leaving the Motorway.

This guide seeks to remove that uncertainty.

Considerations

The first consideration was that it should be a personal and independent assessment of each place, so there was no financial pressure for inclusion or exclusion.

The second was the availability of food at lunchtime, dinner or both. This is not meant to be good food guide, but we sought to find a good standard of pub food.

Another consideration was the availability of bedrooms, which are shown by an illustration of a bed where appropriate.

Lastly, each place should have a friendly or congenial atmosphere.

Pubs of some well known chains have been omitted because we did not feel that they were markedly different from those we were trying to avoid. It is a sad reflection that so many are now owned by national catering groups who impose the same style of decoration, food and furniture throughout their outlets with little regard for local tastes or ways.

Not all Motorways have been included as some did not seem to have any worthwhile stopping places.

Introduction

Facilities.

We have shown on the plans the position of Filling Stations nearby for the benefit of those who like to refuel their cars as well as themselves. We also make special mention of the landlords' attitudes to children and dogs. Under law dogs are not allowed in areas where food is served, Guide dogs being the exception. We also say where arrangements have been made for the disabled, or where access is easy.

Opening/Closing Hours.

Most of the places mentioned open either at 11am or at noon. In the evenings it varies between 5.30pm or 6pm. We thought that the more important time would be when the last orders for food were taken, so these are given for each place. It might be as well to check beforehand.

Prices.

We have tried to give an indication of the price range (using an 8 ounce Sirloin steak as a marker) as follows:

Up to £8	£
£8-£10	££
£10-£15	£££
Over £15	££££

The bedroom charges seem to be in line with that of the food.

Introduction

Motorway Maps and Plans.

We hope that the layout is simple and easy to understand, especially on a dark and rainy night during a long and tiring journey. The Motorways are in numerical order, with a separate section for Scotland.

Each map and plan is orientated with north at the top. The scale varies depending on what has to be shown and how to fit it on to the page.

Motorway Maps. Those junctions with places off them are shown with the appropriate junction numbers whilst the others are shown in grey, so that you can see the distances involved between likely stops.

Junction Plans. Under each junction entry, there is a short introduction of any difficulties you may find (from personal experience) together with a plan. Filling stations are shown thus ⛽. The places included are shown by a letter such as 🅰 on the plan which corresponds with their entry below. Places of interest are given in italics.

Places of Interest.

The names of historic houses or places of interest are given with initials in brackets showing the owners where known. Houses belonging to members of the Historic Houses Association need to be contacted beforehand.

(EH)	*English Heritage.*
(HHA)	*Historic Houses Association.*
(HS)	*Historic Scotland.*
(NT)	*National Trust.*
(NTS)	*National Trust for Scotland.*

Introduction

Entries.

Each entry is given a name, the nearest village
and the contact telephone number. A brief
description is given with mention of bedrooms
where appropriate, attitudes to dogs and children
and last orders for food. Price range is shown by
a £ sign and bedrooms with a bed.

Those places which we thought had particular
appeal have an *. Each entry is illustrated, as a
drawing gives a better idea of the place before
getting off the Motorway.

Assessment

Our opinions were influenced more by the general
appearance, ambiance and atmosphere of the
places, rather than the deep pile carpets or good
food. We also thought strategical positioning of
lesser places might be useful as Comfort Stops.
We hope that the write-ups might be able to give
an impression of a place without being too
specific. As stated those we particularly liked are
marked with an asterisk. Our findings are purely
subjective and you may well disagree with them
or find that places have changed hands in the
meantime or even closed.

If you have any suggestions or find that we have
omitted some which in your opinion should be
included, then please write to us using the blank
listing sheets at the end of the book and receive
not only our thanks but also those of fellow
adventurous motorists.

London to Leeds

Junctions **9** to **48**

The M1 was the first Motorway to be built in the U.K. to motorway standards. The first section of 72 miles was built by Messrs Laing & Son at a cost of £50 million and was completed in 19 months. It was opened in November 1959 by the then Minister of Transport, Ernest Marples, who in real life was a director of a building contracting firm. On the day of the opening an elderly woman crashed her fast Mercedes sports car which resulted in the immediate imposition of speeding restrictions. The final link of the M1, from Leeds to the A1(M) of about 9 miles, was completed in 1999 at a cost of £190 million.

SOUTHERN SECTION   Junctions 9 -18

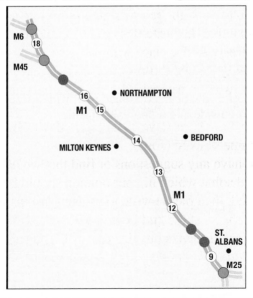

12 Houghton Regis Woburn Flitwick A5120

Toddington is an attractive village with a large green. There are several other pubs in addition to those mentioned. Harlington is harder to find as it is signposted only as Harlington Station.

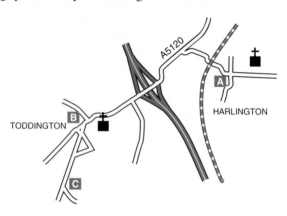

A The Carpenters Arms
Harlington.
☎ 01525 872 384

A cheerful low beamed village pub, with a Beer garden outside and a pool table inside.

Last orders are
2pm and 9pm.
No food on
Sunday evenings
Closed Mondays.

Price ££

 Continued

B The Bell
Toddington
☎ 01525 872 564

A Free House, it is a popular village pub overlooking the green with small areas for eating and a bar. Home cooking and a cheerful atmosphere. Outside seating and a car park at the rear. Children welcome.

Last meal orders
3 and 10.00pm.
No evening meals
on Friday, Saturday
and Sunday.

Price ££

C The Angel
Toddington
☎ 01525 872380

Reputed to date from the 16th century it is owned by Greene King and has moved into the modern age. Bar snacks are available, as is morning coffee and afternoon tea. There is some outside seating. Disabled facilities. Dogs allowed.

Last orders
10.30pm
every day.

Price ££

13 Milton Keynes (S) Bedford A421 Amphill A507 Woburn

The A4102 to Woburn passes through pleasant countryside. Aspley Guise is an attractive village.

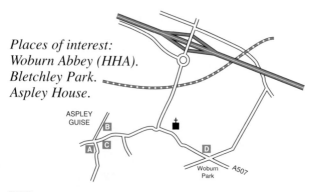

Places of interest:
Woburn Abbey (HHA).
Bletchley Park.
Aspley House.

A Moore Place Hotel
Aspley Guise.
☎ 01908 282 000

A privately owned hotel in a Georgian house built in 1786 with 64 bedrooms mostly in two modern annexes, as well as The Greenhouse Restaurant and a bar. Breakfasts available for passing motorists. Children and dogs welcomed. Facilities for the disabled.

Last orders.
1.45pm and 9.30pm.
No lunch on
Saturdays.

Price £££

to Leeds

 Continued

B The Anchor
Aspley Guise.
☎ 01908 582 177.

It has been a pub for more than 100 years and is owned by the brewery group Charles Wells. It serves morning coffee and afternoon teas as well as bar meals. Children, dogs and coaches are all welcome.
A comfort stop.

Last orders
are 2pm and 9pm.
Closed Sunday
evenings.

Price ££

C Aspleys Bar & Restaurant
Aspley Guise.
☎ 01908 282 877.

Built in 1837 as a coaching inn and called the Bell, it is now a restaurant specialising in Italian food. Garden and car park at rear.
Last orders are at 9.30pm, but 10.00pm on Fridays and
Saturdays.
Closed on
Sundays
and Bank
Holidays.

Price £££

13 Continued

D The White Horse.
Husborne Crawley.
☎ 01525 280 565.

A small pub since 1840 with a pool table and one armed bandits which is now owned by Enterprise. Bar meals served with a Ploughman's Lunch in the summer and a Steak and Kidney Pie in the winter. A comfort stop. There is a childrens playground and outside seating. Children but no dogs.

Last orders 2 and 9pm.
No evening meals on Fridays to Sundays.

Price £

14 Milton Keynes
Newport Pagnell A509

A nondescript Exit in
open countryside.

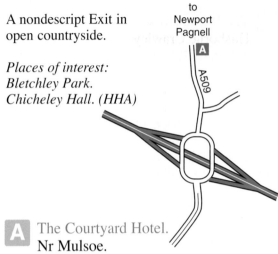

to
Newport
Pagnell

A509

Places of interest:
Bletchley Park.
Chicheley Hall. (HHA)

A The Courtyard Hotel.
Nr Mulsoe.
☎ 01908 613 688.

An 18th century Georgian house forming part
of the Marriott hotel, with 49 double rooms, a
conference centre, brasserie, bars, and a small
leisure centre. Children but no dogs. There is a
bedroom reserved for the disabled. Breakfast
for the passing motorist.

Last orders.
2pm and
10pm
including
Sunday.

Price ££££

15 Northampton (S&E) A508

This Exit has been altered recently to give access to a large industrial estate. However it is worth persevering as Collingtree is an attractive village. It is a bore to get back to the Motorway, as it is a dual carriageway and therefore a one way system to the next roundabout.

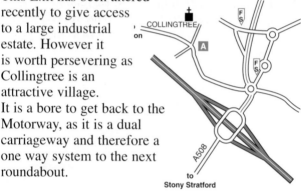

Places of interest: Waterways Museum. Stoke Park Pavilions.

A The Wooden Walls of Old England.
Collingtree.
☎ 01604 762 427.

The name stems from the old beams inside, which came from the timbers of ships. A pleasant and cheerful atmosphere, with a children's playground and a family room. Children and dogs allowed. A car park and beer garden behind.

Last orders for meals 10.30pm.
Closed Mondays.

Price £

to Leeds

16 Northampton Daventry A45

The Exit to Northampton and Daventry.
Follow the dual carriageway to the roundabout
by the Filling Station and then follow the signs
to Kislingbury.

Places of interest: Althorp Hall (HHA)

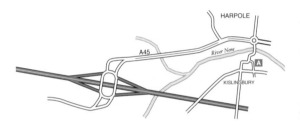

A Cromwell Cottage.
Kislingbury.
☎ 01604 830 288.

Pleasantly situated by the banks of the River
Nene, it is reputedly 600 years old and gets its
name from the fact that Cromwell stayed there.
It is owned by Whitbread and has been
modernised to have the usual large open areas
and restaurant, but with beamed ceilings.
A comfort stop.

It is open from
11.30 onwards
with last order
at 10.00pm.

Price ££

18   Rugby Northampton A428

Pay no attention to the large industrial park to the west but head towards Crick which is a pleasant village.

Places of interest: Althorp Hall. (HHA). Stanford Hall.

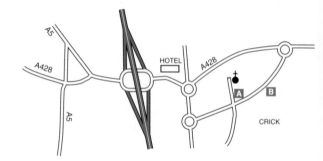

A   The Wheatsheaf.
Crick.
☎ 01788 822 284.

Records date the building to before 1620, but it has been known as the Wheatsheaf since 1742. It has a restaurant and a bar with a beer garden. Dogs allowed but outdoors. A cheerful atmosphere with traditional ales.

Last orders
for meals
2.30 and
9.00pm
8pm Sunday.

Price ££

18 Continued

B The Red Lion.
Crick.
☎ 01788 822 342.

It has been a coaching inn since the early 1700s,
but is said to date from the Norman Conquest.
It is certainly low beamed. Some outside seating
and a car park at the rear. congenial place where
they pride themselves on their Steak Pie.
Traditional ales. Morning coffee served.

Dogs welcome but children only at lunch.
Last Orders. 2pm and 9pm, but 9.30 on
Saturdays. No evening meals on Sundays.

Price ££

MIDDLE SECTION

Junctions 19 - 29

This seems to be a culinary desert with no oasis of peace. However, the magnificent Hardwick Hall, Bolsover Castle and Sutton Scarsdale are a feast for the eyes.

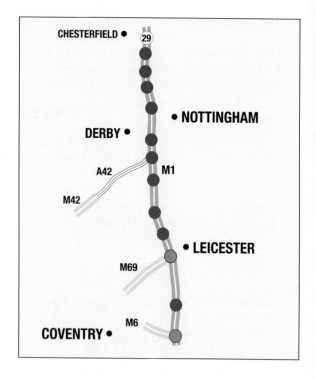

to Leeds

29 | Chesterfield
Mansfield A617

This Exit is studded with the brown signs of the Tourist Board. The sign to Heath can be missed, which is on the way to the gaunt ruins of Sutton Scarsdale.

*Places
of interest;
Hardwick
Hall. (NT)
Bolsover. (EH)
Sutton Scarsdale. (EH)
Chatsworth. (HHA)*

A The Elm Tree.
Heath.
☎ 10246 850 490.

Built about a hundred years ago, it is owned by the Wolverhampton and Dudley Brewery. A friendly welcome with a non-smoking restaurant and bars where they serve home cooked food. There is outside seating where one can have a fine view to the north towards Sutton Scarsdale. Children and dogs are welcome. A comfort stop.

Last orders.
2pm and 9.30pm
Sundays included.

Price £

London

NORTHERN SECTION   Junctions 30 - 48

Certainly not scenic, but interesting, as one drives
through the industrial heartland of this part of
England.

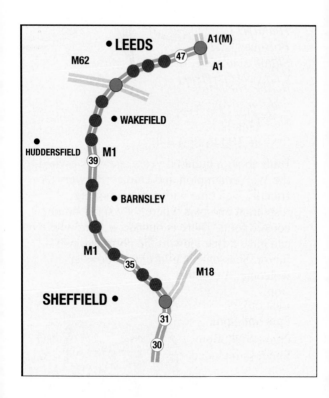

to Leeds

30 Chesterfield Worksop A619
Newark Sheffield A6135

Dual carriageways on each side of the Exit, but
Barlborough is an attractive village when one gets
off the main road.

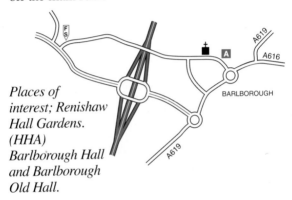

*Places of
interest; Renishaw
Hall Gardens.
(HHA)
Barlborough Hall
and Barlborough
Old Hall.*

A The Rose and Crown.
Barlborough.
☎ 01246 810 364.

The Rose and Crown is signed from the road,
and is close to the old church. It has a childrens
area and a beer garden. The cooking is home
made. Children and dogs permitted but
outdoors.

Last orders.
2pm and 9pm.
No evening
meals on
Monday,
Tuesday
and Sunday.

Price ££

31 Worksop Sheffield A57

A simple Exit, but look out for the road to Aston cum Aughton, when you come off the Exit.

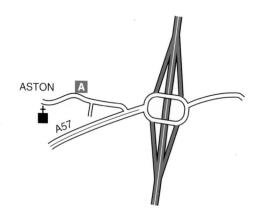

ASTON
A57

A The Yellow Lion.
Aston cum Aughton.
☎ 01142 872 283.

A locals' pub in a fairly built up area, but overlooking the fields. It serves home cooked bar meals and has a children's playground, family room and a beer garden. Dogs allowed. One armed bandits and a pool table.

Last orders.
3pm and 8.45pm.
No evening meals
on Sundays.

Price £

35   Rotherham A629

An easy Exit and one turns right almost immediately, as signed.

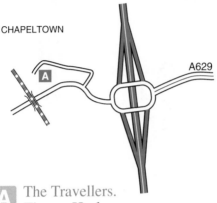

CHAPELTOWN

A

A629

A The Travellers.
Thorpe Hesley.
☎ 01142 467 870.

A surprise, as it is deep in a wood just off the Motorway. It has recently been repainted and renovated and has a large garden at the rear with a childrens playground. Bar meals served. Children and dogs welcome. An outside Wc.

Last orders.
2.30pm and
8.30pm.
No evening
meals
on Sunday
and Monday
evenings.

Price £

39 Wakefield A636 Denby Dale

A fairly unimpressive part of the country, but redolent of its industrial past, especially the part played by waterborne transport.

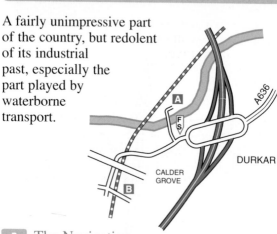

A The Navigation.
Caldergrove.
☎ 01924 274 361.

Situated on the banks of the Calder and Heble Navigation, it is owned by White Rose Inns and must once have been the Dock Masters house, as well as an inn for the boatmen, to judge from the photographs. It serves bar meals and there is a large beer garden on the banks of the Canal. Children and dogs are welcome. Do not be too put off by the car breakers yard opposite.

Last orders are 2pm and 7.45pm on Thursdays, Fridays and Saturdays. Lunches only on Mondays, Tuesdays, Wednesdays and Sundays.

Price £

39 Continued

B The British Oak.
Caldergrave.
☎ 01924 275 286.

Owned by Tetleys, it has a large children's
playground at the rear, as well a beer garden.
It is typical of the many local pubs in the area,
with brown wallpapered ceilings.
Children are obviously welcome but no dogs.
Last orders are 2.15pm and 9.30pm. Sundays
included.

Last orders for food 9.30pm

Price ££

London to Leeds

47 Garforth A642 Tadcaster B1217
The North Wetherby York A64

The last Exit on the M1 before it
merges with a short section of the
new A1 Motorway. Aberford is an
attractive village once on the Great
North Road but now bypassed.

Places of interest: Lotherton Hall.

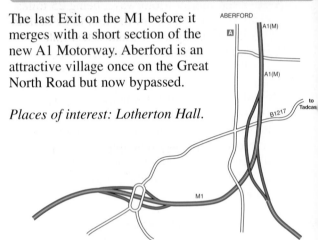

A The White Swan Hotel.
Aberford.
☎ 0113 281 3205.

It has been a Coaching Inn since 1720, when the Great
North Road passed outside it. A rusting sign says that
J. Heaton is licensed to rent post horses. It is a popular
place, full of mementoes and stuffed foxes. There are 2
double and 2 single bedrooms each with a shower. No
dogs. A comfort stop.

Last orders are
2.30pm and 9.30,pm
but until 10.30pm
on Friday and
Saturday nights.

Price ££

London to Canterbury

Junctions 2 to 7

One of the shorter Motorways, being 25 miles in length, and was one of the first to be built in 1963. It was designed to make a fast link between London and the Channel Ports, although the approach to London remained abysmal. It has now been supplanted by the M20, with which one can interchange easily should the traffic become unbearable.
There are major construction works by Rochester, so the M2 is best avoided for the time being.

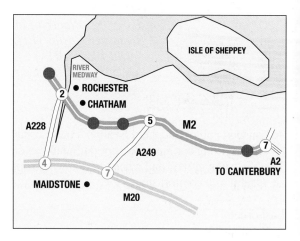

2 Rochester West Mailing A228

Once an easy Exit, it is now the scene of construction work, building the Eurostar bridge over the Medway and the new railtrack.

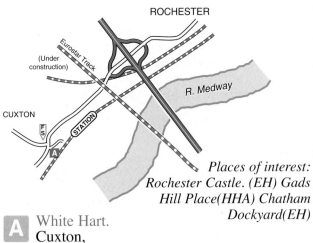

Places of interest: Rochester Castle. (EH) Gads Hill Place(HHA) Chatham Dockyard(EH)

A White Hart.
Cuxton,
☎ 01634 711 857.

A managed pub of Shepherd Neame, it has a restaurant and bars serving bar meals, except on Sunday evenings. There is a playground and a beer garden where dogs can sit. Useful as a comfort stop.

Last orders
2.30 and 9.30pm.

Price ££

to Canterbury

M2

Easy enough to get to Stockbury, as there is a gap in the dual-carriageway, opposite the turning off.

Stockbury features in the Domesday Book as Stochinberge in 1086.

A The Harrow Inn.
Stockbury.
☎ 01795 842 546.

This typical country pub opposite the village green has been there since 1750. It is a Free House and serves cheerful bar meals and Hurlimann Swiss lager every day of the week. There is a beer garden at the rear where dogs and children can roam.

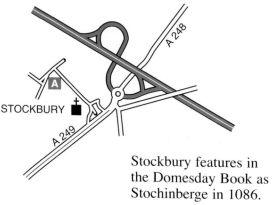

Last orders.
2 and 9.30pm.

Price £££

7   Canterbury A2

The last Exit on the Motorway before it becomes a dual carriageway to Dover. If you are coming from London there is no difficulty in getting to Boughton and rejoining the Dover road on the other side of the village. Coming from Dover, you can either drive up to the roundabout and return, or else bear off the A2 about 2 miles to the south. Boughton is an attractive village with old half-timbered houses in the vernacular style of the Weald.

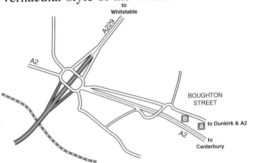

A The Queens Head.
Boughton.
☎ 01227 751 369.

There has been an inn on the site for the past 400 years and is still the locals pub. It serves bar meals, and morning coffee can be had if one is too early for the ferry. One can also pass the time of day playing Bat and Trap a Kentish game. Dogs welcome. A comfort stop.

Last orders. 2.30 and 9pm. No evening meals on Sundays and Mondays.

Price ££

Continued

B The Garden Hotel and Restaurant.
Boughton.
☎ 01227 751 411.

An old 18th Century house, once a soup kitchen in the War, then an Antique shop and for the past ten years a hotel with 10 bedrooms. It has just been totally refurbished. Soup is still on the menu, but there are a great many other choices from the imaginative menu! It has a restaurant and a bar.

Last orders. 2 and 9pm,
but no evening meals on Sundays.

Price ££

Junctions **1** to **4**

The building of the continuation of the Motorway past Winchester in 1994, meant the cutting of a trench through Twyford Down. This caused massive unrest (and cost) by protesters. It might have been cheaper in the long run to have tunnelled through.

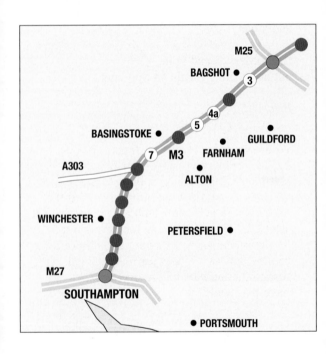

3 Guildford
Bracknell A322 (Woking) ↘

Bagshot has been expanded and therefore you could get lost in the streets. Just keep bearing to the right

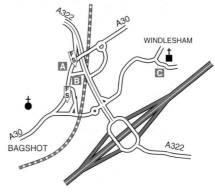

A The Cricketers
Bagshot
☎ 01276 973 196

Now owned by Travellers Inns, it has been entirely modernised with polished wood floors and high backed chairs.It is so named as there is a cricket pavilion and ground behind the hotel, where you can watch a game of cricket, whilst enjoying a drink in the beer garden. There is one single bedroom and 37 double rooms, plus two rooms for the disabled. A restaurant and bars where one can have bar meals.

Last orders.
2.30 and 10.30pm
(10pm on Sundays)

Price £££

3 Continued

B The Old Barn
Bagshot
☎ 01276 476673

An open beamed barn with a collection of farming
artifacts. It is now a restaurant which used to be and
probably still is, much frequented by Officer Cadets
from Sandhurst. It is family owned, where the food is
cooked to order. There is some outside seating,
where children are welcome but no dogs. The
Pantiles club and restaurant, which is owned by the
same people is next door, but the swimming pool of
yesteryear is no more.

Last orders.
2.30 and 9pm
everyday.

Price £££

 Continued

 Half Moon
Windlesham
☎ 01276 473329

A Free House which serves a wide range of traditional food, beers, and fruit wines. As a result it has won the Beer and Food Award and the Surrey, Heath in Bloom Award. Home cooking in the two bars. A large beer garden at the back where dogs are welcome.

Last orders 2.15 and 9.30pm.
No evening meals on Sundays.

Price £££

M3

London

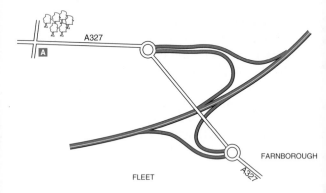

4a Farnborough (W) A327
Fleet B3013

A simple exit and the pub is easy to find.

*Places of interest: Napoleon III's Mausoleum,
Farnborough. Airborne Forces Museum. Aldershot.*

A327

FARNBOROUGH

A327

FLEET

 Crown and Cushion
Yateley
☎ 01252 545253

An attractive rural pub in a wooded area on the way
to Yateley Common. It serves traditional meals in the
bars and carvery, or else in the beer garden, which
has heaters should the weather be inclement. Dogs
welcome.

Last orders
2 and 8.30pm
No evening meals
on Sundays.

Price ££

5 Farnham A287

No real difficulty with this exit, but take the road off the southern roundabout to North Warnborough.

Places of interest:
Farnham
Castle
Keep.
Old Basing
House.

WARNBOROUGH GREEN

A287

to Guildford

to Odiham

A Blubeckers Mill House Restaurant
North Warnborough
☎ 01256 702 953

As the name suggests, this was once an old water mill and the mill pond makes an attractive setting for the restaurant, which is olde worlde. There is a playground, a family room and outside seating. Children welcome but no dogs. The food is imaginative if one likes sparklers on the ice cream.
It has recently changed hands.

Last orders
1.45 and
9.45pm

Price £££

London

7 **Basingstoke A30**
Newbury (A339)

Not a difficult exit and in fact one can get from one
pub to the other under the Motorway should one of
them be full.

Places of interest: Northington Grange (EH)

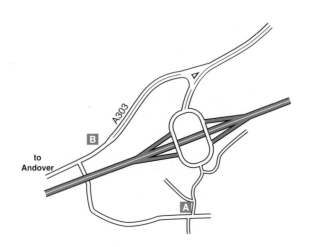

7 Continued

Queen Inn
Dummer
☎ 01256 397 367

A family owned pub. It gets its name from the fourth wife of Henry VIII, Anne of Cleves the Mare of Flanders, although it is only 200 years old. Its speciality is Steak and Kidney Pie for which people come from far and near. There is a garden at the back where dogs are welcome.

Last orders 2.30 and 10pm on Thursday, Friday and Saturday 9.30 otherwise.

Price £££

Sun Inn
Nr Dummer
☎ 01256 397 234

Once a Coaching inn on the old Andover road, it is now owned by a group, but still makes a speciality of its pies and casseroles in the restaurant or in the bars. It has outside seating and a beer garden where dogs are welcome and a playground which children may use. A comfort stop.

Last orders 2.30 and 9pm (9.30pm on Fridays and Saturdays)

Price ££

M4

London

Junctions **1** to **49**

The M4, which is 121 miles long, is the fourth
longest Motorway in the UK. The first section, the
Chiswick Flyover, was opened in 1959 by a blonde
starlet, and the last part to be completed was in 1973.
It may be continued to Fishguard at some future date,
instead of terminating in a rather bleak part of South
Wales. It passes through some of the most varied
scenery in Southern England.

EASTERN SECTION   **Junctions 8/9 - 14**

This section passes Windsor Castle and follows
along the Thames Valley. Then it climbs up towards
the Marlborough Downs.

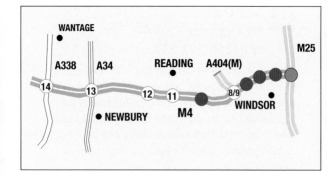

to South Wales

8&9 Maidenhead Windsor A308
Bracknell A308
Henley High Wycombe A4(M)

Coming off at the Exit, it is a Motorway spur to
the roundabout. Then follow the signs to
Holyport and turn left at the village green. For
the Shire Horse, take the A404 (M) and turn left
at the roundabout.

Places of Interest: Dorney Court.(HHA)
Windsor Castle. (HM The Queen).

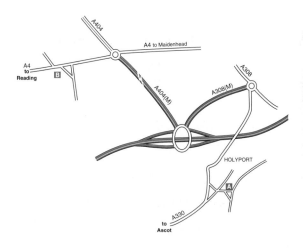

8&9 Continued

 The Belgian Arms.
Holyport,
☎ 01628 634 468.

On the edge of the village green by a duck pond which ducks still use, the pub is a haven of tranquility in an area one would assume to be overpopulated. A good surrounding and good food. There is a large garden by the pond where one can si in the summer and dogs can play.

Last orders.
2 and 9.30pm.
No evening meals
on Sundays.

Price £££

 The Shire Horse.
Littlewick Green
☎ 01628 825 335.

The pub, which is part of Scottish and Newcastle. In an open beamed and brick area, it serves Bar meals and there is a beer garden and children's playground. No dogs. Facilities for the disabled.

Last orders.
All day to 10pm.
(9pm on Sundays)

Price ££

to South Wales

11 Basingstoke A33 Reading

At the roundabout turn left to Three Mile Cross, but avoid getting onto the dual carriageway.

Places of interest: Stratfield Saye.(HHA) Silchester.(Calleva Atrebartum)

READING

SHINFIELD

THREE MILE CROSS

A33

A The Swan
Three Mile Cross,
☎ 01189 883 674

Traditional old pub and a restaurant for lunches on weekdays, serving bar meals with its home cooking. There is some outside seating and a beer garden beyond.The resident Irish Wolf Hound keeps control of delinquent children.

Last orders
All day
to 10pm
every day.

Price ££

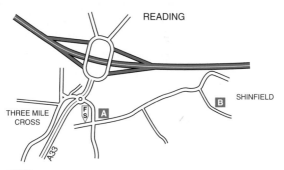

 **Continued**

B L'Ortolan Restaurant
Shinfield.
☎ 01189 883 783

An old vicarage, with a large garden, now converted
to a comfortable restaurant, specialising in classical
French cuisine. A patio where you can have a drink
before lunch.

Last orders
2.30 and 9.30pm
No evening meals on Sundays.

Price ££££*

12 Theale
Reading A4

Turn off the Motorway onto the A4 to Newbury.
At the roundabout turn right to Theale, which is
a surprisingly attractive little town, so named as
it was the second wagoners stop out of London
and was called The Ale. It certainly seems to
have more than its fair share of pubs and hotels,
so if the two mentioned below are full, there are
probably alternatives.

Places of Interest.
Engelfield House
Garden.(HHA)
Basildon
Park.(NT)

A The Volunteer.
Theale.
☎ 01189 302 489.

Traditional old pub, serving bar meals with its
home cooking. There is outside seating, and a
car park at the rear. An interesting collection of
military and sporting prints.
No dogs indoors.

Last orders
2.15 and 9pm
No evening
meals
on Sundays.

Price ££

12 Continued

B The Old Lamb Hotel
Theale.
☎ 01189 302 357.

The house dates from 1487. It is privately owned, with 28 single bedrooms, mostly in the annexe at the rear by the carpark. A restaurant but only for the residents at dinner. Children welcome.

Last orders
are normally 9.30pm

Price ££

13 Oxford Newbury A34

Take the Oxford road and the first slip road off
the dual carriageway to the north and head for
Chievely.

Places of interest:
Didcot Railway
Centre

A Ye Olde Red Lion.
Chievely.
☎ 01635 248 379.

Basically a village pub, it has a restaurant and a
bar, with benches outside for those wanting
fresh air. Home cooking is the order of the day.
Children welcome. There is a resident dog.

Last orders.
2.30 and
9.30pm
every day.

Price ££

13 Continued

B The Red House
Marsh Benham.
☎ 01635 582 017

A privately owned elegant restaurant with an adjoining bar, in a thatched house. Outside seating in a garden and its own carpark. They specialise in fish tinged with French cuisine as the Manager is a Breton. Children and dogs welcome preferably outside. Well worth the additional minutes to get there.

Last meal orders
2.15 and 10pm
No evening meals on Sunday. Closed Mondays.

Price £££*

to South Wales

14 Hungerford Wantage A338

An easy exit. Follow the sign to Lambourn for the Pheasant Inn.

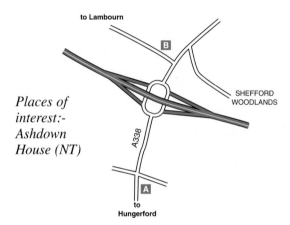

to Lambourn

B

SHEFFORD
WOODLANDS

*Places of
interest:-
Ashdown
House (NT)*

A338

A

to
Hungerford

A Tally Ho.
Hungerford Newtown
☎ 01488 682 312.

A friendly roadside pub since 1875, which serves bar meals and morning coffee for those in need. Some outside seating and dogs are welcome.

Last orders.
2.30 and 9.30pm.
(9pm on Sundays).

Price ££

14 Continued

  The Pheasant Inn
Woodlands St Mary
☎ 01488 648 284

It has recently been renovated to include a restaurant with an excellent chef. It is a pleasant stopover, especially for the racing fraternity. Outside seating in a garden.

Last food orders.
2.30 and 9.30pm.
No evening meals
on Sundays.

Price £££*

to South Wales

MIDDLE SECTION   Junctions 15 - 23

The motorway descends from the chalk downs to Junction 15, and from there into Cotswold country. In 1996 the second Severn Bridge was completed to cope with the increased traffic. The older bridge crossing was then renamed the M48, and the new section became the M4. The M49 links the M4 to Avonmouth and is best avoided if one is seeking culinary diversions.

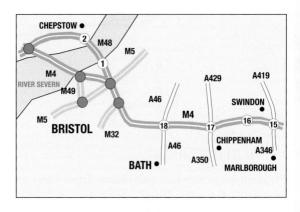

M4   London

15   Swindon A419
          Marlborough A364

There is a clutch of pubs in this area, who probably did a roaring trade here when Chiseldon was an Airforce base, and then an American military hospital.

Places of Interest: Avebury Stone Circle. (EH)
Ashdown House (NT)
Waylands Smithy.
Barbury Castle.

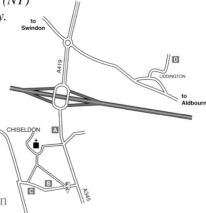

A Plough Inn
Badbury.
☎ 01793 740 342.

Pleasant busy wayside pub dating from 1864 and part of Arkells Brewery. It has a restaurant and a bar, childrens playground, beer garden and its own car park. Coffee is available for the passing motorist. Dogs are welcome.

Last orders.
2 and 9.00pm.

Price ££

15 Continued

B Chiseldon House Hotel.
Chiseldon.
☎ 01793 741 010.

A fine 19th Century Manor house, which became a privately owned hotel about ten years ago, and is getting increasingly busy with conferences and receptions. It has one single and 20 double rooms, extensive gardens and a peaceful setting. Children and dogs are welcome. It has the Orangery Restaurant and a bar. Morning coffee for the casual visitor.

Last orders
2 and 9.15pm
every day

Price £££

C Patriots Arms.
Chiseldon.
☎ 01793 740 331.

Has been a pub since 1840 and is now a Free House, with a single and a double bedroom, a restaurant and bar. A beer garden, children's playground with a wooden ship and a family room for wet days. A large carpark at rear. Dogs however are not welcome.

Last orders.
2 and 9pm
every day.

Price ££

15 Continued

 The Village Inn.
Liddington.
☎ 01793 790 314.

A creeper clad village inn, which serves real ales and bar meals, with their Steak and Ale Pie top of the menu. Children over 8 only and dogs to be kept outdoors. However it is a comfortable, busy and friendly place.

Last orders.
2 and 9.30pm
(9.00 on Sundays).

Price ££

to South Wales

16 Swindon Wootton Bassett Calne A3102

An uninspiring Exit, but easy enough to find the pub, which is before you get into Wootton Bassett.

Places of Interest: Lydiard Park.(Swindon B.C.)

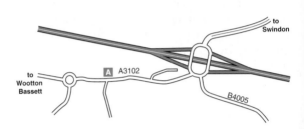

A Sally Pussey's Inn.
Nr Wootton Bassett,
☎ 01793 852 430

Do not be too put off by the formidable woman portrayed on the inn sign, as the welcome inside is friendly. It has a Steak and Carvery Restaurant as well as a bar, which also serves bar meals. There is a beer garden where dogs are allowed. Breakfast from 8am.

Last orders.
9.30pm.
(9pm on Sundays).

Price ££

17 Chippenham A350 Cirencester A429

Most of the pubs are easy to find, but the Hit and Miss in Kington Langley could be missed which would be a great pity. Take the narrow road when you come off the roundabout.

Places of Interest:
Bowood House.(HHA)
Lacock Abbey.(NT)
Corsham Court. (HHA)

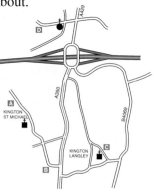

A The Jolly Huntsman,
Kington St Michael,
☎ 01249 750 305

A popular locals' pub in this attractive village. Well known for its Real Ales of which there are at least 6 different varieties and as a result it has been in the Good Beer Guide for the past ten years. There are 6 double bedrooms above for those who might wish to drink to the full. Log fires and home made bar meals. Some outside seating and dogs are welcome by the amiable owners, who stay open for 365 days of the year.

Last orders.
2 and 10pm
(9pm on Sundays)

Price ££*

17 Continued

B The Plough,
Kington Langley
☎ 01249 750255

An old 18th Century house, which could have
been a coaching stop. It is a Free House and
caters for the business community of
Chippenham, as well as passing trade. There is
a modern conservatory which is the restaurant,
but bar meals are also served. Outside seating
where dogs are allowed. It has recently
changed hands.

Last orders.
2.00 and 10.00pm.
(10pm on Saturdays
and Sundays)

Price £££

C The Hit and Miss.
Kington Langley
☎ 01249 758 830

A popular village pub dating from the 18th
Century in the middle of this scattered hamlet.
There is a friendly welcome to all including
dogs and it has an imaginative menu. A good
ambiance. Some outside seating for summer
use. It specialises in sea food.

Last orders.
2.30 and 9.30pm.
(8.30pm on Sundays)

Price ££*

17 Continued

D Stanton Manor Hotel
Stanton St Quintin.
.☎ 01666 837 552.

A privately owned hotel, set in 7 acres of garden,
which has recently changed hands. The new owners,
Duncan and Linda Hickling, have been carrying out
improvements to the house and grounds and as a
result, it is a comfortable and friendly place, with
some 24 bedrooms, most in a modern annexe. It has
a Croquet Lawn and for the more sportive, a Golf
Course.
No children, but dogs by arrangement. Bar meals are
served, and there is the Burghley Restaurant, so
named as the house was once owned by Queen
Elizabeth's Chief Minister.

Last orders. 2 and 9.30pm

*Price £££ **

18   Bath Stroud A46

An easy Exit and
not difficult to
find the various
places.

*Places of
Interest: Dyrham
Park (NT)
Horton Court
(NT)*

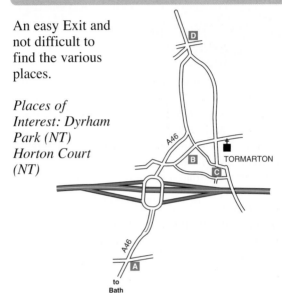

A The Crown Inn
Nr Hinton.
☎ 01225 891 231.

An old Coaching Inn since 1703, it is still
welcoming with open fires and a restaurant and
bars where they specialise in home cooked,
Steak and Mushroom Pie. There is a children's
playground and a beer garden where dogs are
allowed.

Last orders 2.15
and 9.30pm.
(10pm on Fridays
and Saturdays)

Price ££

18 Continued

 B

The Compass Inn
Tormarton.
☎ 01454 218 242.

A privately owned hotel, restaurant and pub. It
started life in 1760 and has been growing in
popularity ever since. Today it has 26 bedrooms, a
restaurant and bars. Perry or local Cider is available,
as well as a wide range of South African wines.
A large garden where
dogs are welcome.

Last orders
All day until 10.30pm
(10pm on Sundays).

Price £££

 C

The Portcullis Inn
Tormarton.
☎ 01454 218 263.

A friendly, old fashioned, privately owned village
pub, with 6 double bedrooms. There is a restaurant
and a bar which serves an excellent Steak and
Kidney Pie, so much so that it is now an essential
stopping off point for Czech tourists. A beer garden
where children are welcome, but the resident
dog is not too keen on
canine visitors.

Last orders.
2.30 and 9.45pm
every day.

Price ££

18 Continued

D Cross Hands Hotel
Old Sodbury.
☎ 01454 313 000.

An old Coaching Inn which used to be a livery
stable for those coming down for a day out with
the Beaufort. It has an ingenious mix of new
and old and the 9 double and 6 single bedrooms
still reflect those bygone days as not all of them
have bathrooms attached. There is a restaurant
and bars where morning coffee and afternoon
teas are still served. A claim to fame is that the
Queen had to spend the night there in 1981
when marooned in a snow storm. Dogs are
welcome, especially Corgis.

Last orders. 2.30
and 10.30pm
(10pm on Sundays).

Price £££

WELSH SECTION
Junctions 23a - 48

As the map suggests there are few places where it is worth leaving the motorway. This is a pity as Cardiff has some fine buildings, especially the Castle and nearby there is Castell Coch both restored by the Marquis of Bute with the help of the architect William Burges in the nineteenth Century.

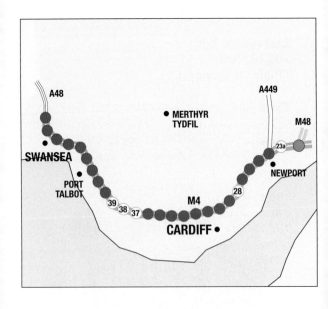

to South Wales

M4

23a Magor B4245

A slightly complicated Exit. The approach to the village can confuse the direction to the pub.

Places of Interest: Penhow Castle (HHA)

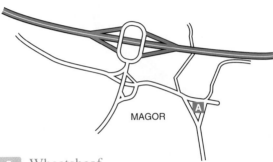

MAGOR

A Wheatsheaf.
Magor
☎ 01633 880 608.

Some two hundred years old, it has 5 double bedrooms. Downstairs, there is a large open plan restaurant and bars, where home made food is served. There is some outside seating. Dogs are permitted.

Last Orders.
2 and 9.30pm.
9.45pm on
Saturdays and
closed on Sunday
evenings.

Price £

28 Newport A48 Caerphilly A468

Once off the motorway follow the signs to Tredegar House.

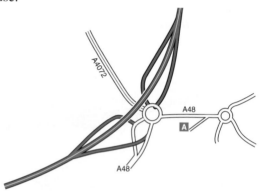

A The Brewhouse Tearoom
Tredegar House
☎ 01633 817 279.

Tredegar House, which is a member of the HHA, is open to the public from Easter to the end of September. The Brewhouse Tearoom is really a cafe, but serves light lunches as well as morning coffee and cream teas. A slightly different atmosphere from the usual Motorway stopover.

Last orders
5pm Wednesdays
to Sundays
Closed Mondays
and Tuesdays.

Price £

to South Wales

M4

37 Porthcawl Pyle A4229

Turn left past an ex Filling Station. The pub cannot be seen from the main road. A comfort stop.

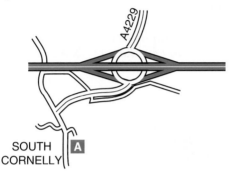

SOUTH
CORNELLY | **A**

A Three Horse Shoes.
South Cornelly
☎ 01656 740 037.

It has been a pub for the past two hundred years and at some point was enlarged by including the next door cottage. It has a restaurant and bars, where home roasts have pride of place on the menu. A playground and a beer garden. Dogs are welcome.

Last orders.
2 and 9.30pm
(8.45pm on
Sundays).

Price £

38 Port Talbot A48

Going east there is no problem about exiting and
entering again, but driving west, one has to take the
dual carriageway for a short distance before joining
the Motorway again.

Places of interest: Margam Castle (HHA)
The Stones Museum. Margam Abbey.

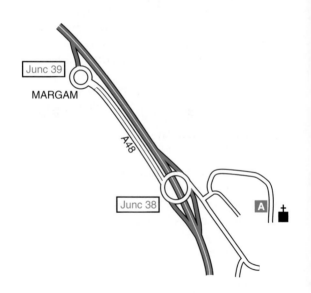

38 Continued

A The Abbots Kitchen and Restaurant.
Margam.
☎ 01639 871 184.

A haven of peace shielded from the steel works
in Port Talbot by woodland. The Restaurant is
in the stables of what was once Margam House
before it was demolished. The whole area was
part of an Early Norman Abbey, The church
was 'restored' by the Victorians, but
nevertheless still a fine building, where services
are still held. Nearby is the Stones Museum
with a good collection of inscribed Celtic
stones.
If refreshment is required, the Abbots Kitchen,
provides you with tea, coffee and cakes or a
light lunch until 4pm.
Dogs and children welcome.

Last orders. 2.30pm on Sundays.

Price £

M5

Birmingham

Junctions **1** to **31**

The M5 is 168 miles in length and was built in
sections, the first part being completed in 1969 and
the last in 1976. It was designed to link the Midlands
with the South West, via Bristol. It is one of the few
Motorways which has no connection with London.
Considering that it passes through some of the
prettiest of the English countryside, it is poorly
served for looking after the needs of motorists.

NORTHERN SECTION - Junctions 1 -10

A boring stretch of motorway until one gets south of
Worcester.

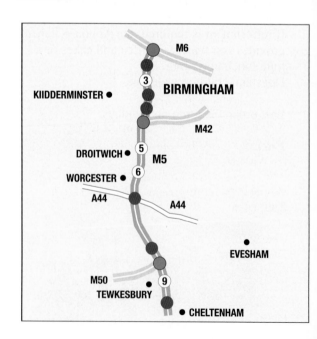

to Exeter

3 Birmingham (W and Cen) A456 Kidderminster

A boring but straightforward Exit. Just follow the dual carriageway until you see the pub. You will have to get back to the Exit by going round the roundabout. A comfort stop.

Places of Interest:
Hagley Hall. (HHA)

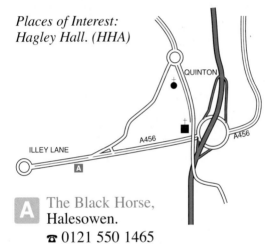

QUINTON

A456

A456

ILLEY LANE

A

A The Black Horse,
Halesowen.
☎ 0121 550 1465

An outlet of The Spirit Group, it is however a cheerful stopover. Outside seating, where dogs are allowed.
It serves in-house created meals in a peaceful atmosphere of (at present) William Morris wallpaper.

Last orders.
2 and 10pm
(9.30 On
Sundays.

Price ££

 Droitwich Bromsgrove A38

The roundabouts tend to confuse but look out for the signs to Droitwich.

Places of Interest:
Hanbury Hall (NT)

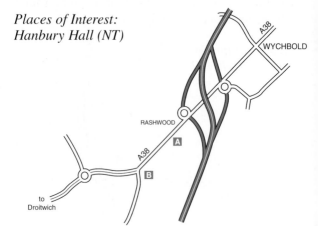

A Robin Hood.
Rashwood,
☎ 01527 861 931.

A Bass owned pub, it is well known to the passing motorist. Outside seating and a beer garden at the rear, where dogs are allowed. There are facilities for the disabled.

Last orders.
9.30pm from
Mondays to Fridays.
10pm on Saturdays
and 9pm on Sundays.

Price ££

5 Continued

B Chateau Impney.
Nr Droitwich,
☎ 01905 774 411.

An amazing French edifice in the middle of
England. It has amongst many other attractions,
14 single and 100 double bedrooms; two
Restaurants, a Carvery and Lounge Bars. It is
privately owned and prides itself on its cuisine.
There is a golf course nearby for those wishing
to work off their lunch. No dogs.

Last orders.
2 and 8.30pm(9pm on Sundays).

Price ££££

M5

Birmingham

6   Kidderminster A449
Evesham A4538

Follow the plan so as not to
overshoot the turning to the right.

Places of interest:
Worcester Cathedral.
Dyson Perrins Museum
(Royal Worcester
porcelain)
Droitwich Spa.

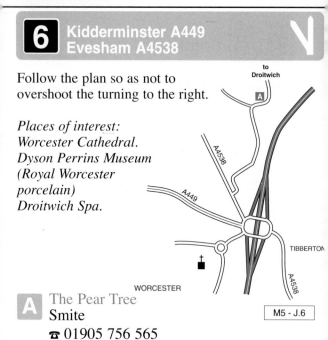

A The Pear Tree
Smite
☎ 01905 756 565

A family owned 24 bedroom hotel and conference
centre, which was converted and enlarged some ten
years ago. The original house dating from the 18th
century is now where you can have bar meals. Fresh
fish a speciality. No dogs. Breakfast for the passing
traveller.

Last food orders.
2.30 and 9.30pm.

Price £££

to Exeter

9 Tewkesbury A438
Evesham A46

A simple Exit. Just keep going until you see the tower of the Abbey. It is a picturesque old market town with some fine buildings.

Places of Interest: Tewkesbury Abbey

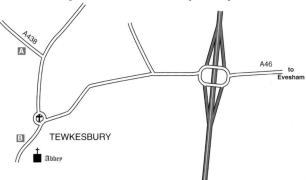

A Ye Olde Black Bear.
Tewkesbury,
☎ 01684 292 202.

Said to be the oldest pub in Gloucestershire, dating from 1308. It has a beer garden at the rear by the lower Avon Navigation Canal where dogs are allowed. Bar meals are served throughout the day.
A comfort stop.

Last orders.
9pm, but no evening meals on Sunday.

Price ££

9 Continued

B The Royal Hop Pole.
Tewkesbury
☎ 01684 293 236.

It is a comfortable old fashioned hotel. No one seems to know the origin of the name, but it dates from the 15th century. It is also famous as the place where Dickens wrote that Pickwick spent the night there! There are 23 double and 6 single bedrooms facing onto a garden at the rear. A restaurant and a bar looks after the inner man, or should one say person.

Last orders. 2 and 9pm.(9.30pm on Fridays and Saturdays) No evening meals on Sundays.

Price £££

to Exeter

MIDDLE SECTION   Junctions 13 -21

The northern half passes through attractive
countryside, but at the intersection with the M4
one starts to get slowed by increasing traffic,
especially near the bridge over the River Avon.

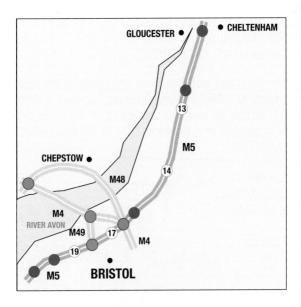

13 Stroud A419

An easy Exit.

Places of Interest:
Hardwicke Court.
(HHA)
Wildfowl
and Wetlands
Trust.(Slimbridge)

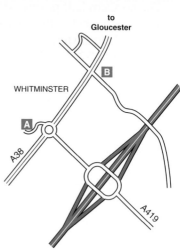

A Frombridge Mill
Whitminster.
☎ 01452 741 796.

The old water mill has been converted a few years go
to form an extensive area serving bar meals all day as
well as a restaurant, on the banks of the river Frome.
Dogs are allowed outdoors. There are facilities for
the disabled.

Last orders.
3 and 9.30pm
(9pm on Sundays)

Price ££

13 Continued

B The Old Forge
Whitminster.
☎ 01452 741 306.

The building is dated 1604 and must have been a smithy, if the name is to be believed. It is a Free House and has a friendly atmosphere. It has a small low beamed restaurant. There is outside seating and dogs are welcome.

Last orders. 2.30 and 9.30pm.
No evening meals on Sundays.

Price ££ *

14 Thornbury Dursley B4509

An uncomplicated Exit.

Places of Interest:
Berkeley Castle.(HHA)

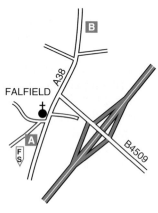

A The Huntsman.
Falfield.
☎ 01454 260 239.

A Managed House of Whitbreads. It was probably a wayside stop on the old coaching road. There is outside seating in a garden where dogs are permitted, but no children's playground. Inside there is a restaurant and bars which serve bar meals.

Last orders.
2.30 and 9pm.
(9.30 on Fridays
and Saturdays)

Price ££

14 Continued

B The Gables
Falfield.
☎ 01454 260 502.

The Gables was once a wayside pub. It is now a modern design and build hotel with a bar, Restaurant and a Fitness Gym for those wanting a workout or relaxing from a conference there. It has 46 bedrooms and will serve breakfast to passing travellers. It is a comfortable stopover.

Last orders.
2pm for bar meals only
9pm in the bar and restaurant.

Price ££

17   Bristol Clifton A4018

Easy enough to find the way, especially if in need of a comfort stop. Good view towards the Severn Bridges.

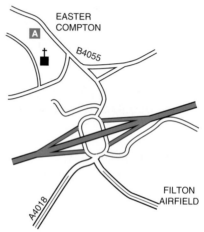

A The Fox.
Easter Compton
☎ 01454 632 220.

A well run pub with a garden and children's playground. Morning coffee can be had if in a rush.

Last orders.
2 and 9.30pm.
(No evening
meals
on Sundays).

Price ££

to Exeter

19 Clifton
Portishead A369

The Rudgeleigh Inn is easy to find, but the
Priory, will require more effort, especially as it
is a narrower road.

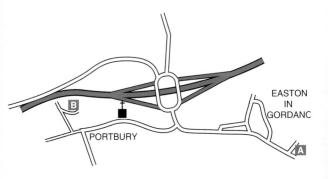

A Rudgeleigh Inn.
Easton in Gordano.
☎ 01275 372 363.

It is family owned pub, with a large collection
of jugs hanging from the beams. Children and
dogs are welcome. There is outside seating and
morning coffee and afternoon teas are also
served.

Last orders.
Through the day
to 10pm (9.30pm
on Sundays).

Price ££

19 Continued

A The Priory.
Portbury,
☎ 01275 378 411.

So named from the Priory which used to stand across the road. Once an imposing Georgian house it has now been converted into a folksy layout of beamed eating areas. There is outside seating and a garden, where children and dogs on leads are allowed.

Last orders.
10pm and 9.30
on Sundays.

Price ££

SOUTHERN SECTION Junctions 22 -31

This section starts in the Mendip Hills and then crosses over the flat fenlands around Sedgemoor. After Taunton the motorway passes through undulating countryside until the sea, south of Exeter.

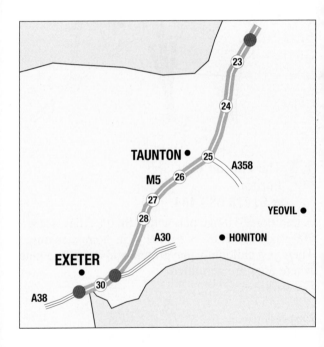

Birmingham

23 Bridgwater A38
Glastonbury Wells (A39)

The Puriton Inn is signed just off the Exit,
on the left.

*Places of Interest: Glastonbury Abbey.
Wells Cathedral*

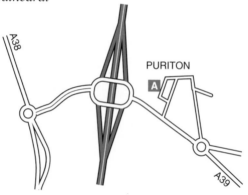

A The Puriton Inn,
Puriton,
☎ 01278 683 464.

A traditional village pub with a Skittle Alley, some
200 years old. It takes a pride in its home cooking.
There is a children's playground and outside seating,
where dogs are permitted.
Car park.

Last orders.
2.30 and 9.30pm.
(9pm on Sundays)

Price £

to Exeter

24 Bridgewater A38
Minehead

The Exit is easy enough, but the road to
Huntworth is twisty and narrow - keep on over a
narrow wooden bridge.

Places of Interest:
Maunsel
Grange Garden.
(HHA)

A The Boat and Anchor Inn.
Huntworth.
☎ 01278 662 473.

The reason for the name soon becomes apparent
as the Inn is on the banks of the Bridgewater
and Taunton Canal. There is a large dining area
and bar. You can sit out on the lawn by the
canalside. Coffee and afternoon tea are also
served to thirsty bargees. Dogs and children
welcome. It also has overnight accommodation
by way of 2 double and a single bedroom. The
noise from the nearby M5 tends to overcome the
peaceful idyll.

Last orders
12.30 and 9pm
every day.

Price £

M5   Birmingham

24   Continued

B The Compass Tavern.
North Petherton
☎ 01278 662 283.

A tenanted pub, which specialises in home cooking
in a large open beamed dining area. There is outside
seating in a garden. Pay heed to the notices to mind
your step or mind your head. Children allowed.

Last orders.
2.45 and 9.15 inc Sundays.

Price ££

25 Taunton Honiton Yeovil Weymouth A358

An easy Exit, being the main route to Taunton. Follow the signs to Ilminster, and the Blackbrook Tavern is just to the left, on the Ilminster road.

Places of Interest:
Hestercombe
House Gardens. (HHA)

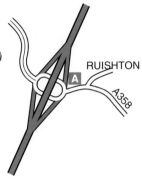

RUISHTON

A358

A Blackbrook Tavern.
Ruishton
☎ 01823 443 121.

A popular and busy pub, of beams and bricks, on the outskirts of Taunton, with 38 double bedrooms, a restaurant and bars. It also serves breakfasts.. There is a children's playground as well as outside seating. Dogs are not welcome.

Last orders .
Through the day
to 10pm
but 9.30pm on
Sundays.

Price ££

26 Wellington A38
Taunton

Turn right on the roundabout on the A38 if going to
The Blackbird, otherwise go straight on to
Wellington,which is a pleasant country town but
nothing special in the way of places to eat. The
return to the Motorway from the Blackbird via West
Buckland is not recommended, as the roads are
narrow and one could get lost.

Places of Interest:
Cothay
Manor
Gardens
(HHA)

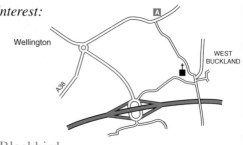

 The Blackbird.
West Buckland.
☎ 018223 461 273.

A Free House, it prides itself on the home cooking,
served in the restaurant, with lace table cloths, and in
the bar. It also has 2 bed rooms for the overnight
motorist. Outside there is a beer garden but dog
owners are warned that there are two large resident
dogs. Children welcome.

Last orders.
2 and 9.30pm.
No evening meals
on Sundays.

Price ££ *

27 Tiverton Barnstaple A361
Wellington A38

Getting there is easy enough but the return is more difficult, with what seems to be a needlessly complicated system of roundabouts.

Places of Interest: Knightshayes Court.(NT)

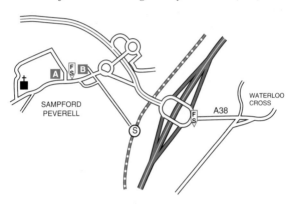

A The Globe Inn.
Sampford Peverell
☎ 01884 821 214.

A popular pub, with a restaurant and bars as well as 6 double bedrooms. There is a children's playground and a beer garden at the rear. Dogs are welcome, and there are facilities for the disabled. A skittle alley for use on wet days.

Last orders.
2 and 10pm
every day.

Price £

27 Continued

B The Parkway House Hotel
Sampford Peverell
☎ 01884 820 255

An unassuming building with a large garden, but
inside an airy and well furnished conservatory
restaurant and ten bedrooms. Children welcome, but
no dogs.

Last food orders. 2.15 and 9.30pm
No dinner on Sunday.

Price ££

28 Cullompton B3181 Honiton A373

Slightly complicated by having a Motorway
Service Station just off the Exit. There is also
another filling station on the way into
Cullompton, which is an attractive town. You
may miss the road back to the Exit by heading
off north.
Both could be treated
as comfort stops.

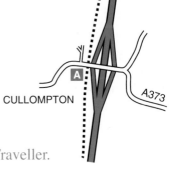

CULLOMPTON

A373

A The Weary Traveller.
Cullompton.
☎ 01884 323 17.

Certainly the closest and easiest to find from the
Motorway. It was a Georgian house, but is now
converted to modern pub use with a large dining
area and bar. There is a large garden at the rear
which includes a childrens playground and at
present a large lorry trailer! A comfort stop.
Dogs are not welcome.

Last orders.
2 and 9pm.
Closed Monday
evenings.

Price ££

M5

Birmingham

28 Continued

B Manor House Hotel
Cullompton.
☎ 01884 322 281.

A 17th Century town house which must have been of
some importance. It is now privately owned with part
being a hotel with 9 bedrooms and a restaurant, the
other part being a public bar, which has not been
renovated. Outside seating and a car park at the rear.

Last orders.
2.30pm and 9.30pm
Lunch only on Sundays.

Price £

to Exeter

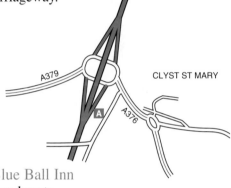

30 Exmouth Sidmouth A376 Dawlish

The village is not difficult to find. To get to the Blue Ball Inn, you will have to go up to the roundabout and return as there is no break in the dual carriageway.

A379

CLYST ST MARY

A376

A Blue Ball Inn
Sandygate
☎ 01392 877 678.

An attractive 18th Century pub in a quiet lane, with scrubbed tables, tiled floors and low beamed ceiling. It specialises in home cooking. Morning Coffee and afternoon teas can also be had. There is a children's playground and a large garden, but dogs are not welcome. It is about to be enlarged.

Last orders. 2.30 and 9.30pm (9pm on Sundays).

Price ££

Junctions 1 to 44

The M6 is one of the longest Motorways, being some 180 miles in length. It was built over a period of years, starting in 1962 and the last section was finished in 1972. The link over the Scottish Border connecting up with the M74 is still to be completed.

SOUTHERN SECTION   Junctions 1 - 14

This section of the motorway is dull and when combined with the inevitable snarl-up at Spaghetti Junction, it becomes downright tedious. It improves south of Stafford.

to Carlisle

1 Lutterworth Rugby A426

Take care not to
miss the sign
saying
Churchover.
If you do,
continue
for half a mile
and take the next
turning. Open
rolling country
and a quiet village.

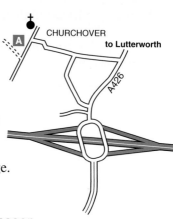

A The Haywaggon,
Churchover,
☎ 01788 832 307.

A 300 year old house converted to a restaurant
and pub. It has a large dining area with beamed
ceilings and bar, with a further restaurant in a
conservatory. A childrens playground but no
dogs. The owner is Italian and specialises in
Italian food, especially fish.

Last orders.
2 and 10pm.
Closed Sunday
Evenings.

Price ££

11 Wolverhampton Cannock A460
Telford (M54)

On the way to Shareshill there is a filling station
but it only sells diesel.
For those driving from the north and wanting to go
to Shrewsbury, turn off here to get to the M54.

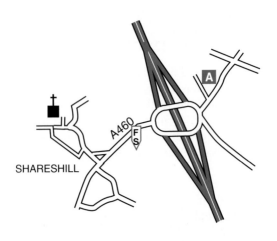

 Continued

 The Wheatsheaf
Laney Green
☎ 01922 412 304.

An old road side pub, but now more
modernised, with a conservatory style dining
area. Bar meals served. Childrens playground, a
garden and plenty of parking.

Last orders.
2 and 8.30pm.
Closed Sunday
Evenings.

Price ££

MIDDLE SECTION   Junctions 15 - 32

The Southern part of this section passes through the pleasant Cheshire countryside. North of the Manchester Ship Canal, the surroundings are more crowded, mingled with motorways.

to Carlisle

17 Congleton Sandbach A534

The Chimney House Hotel is further than one
thinks, but look out for Church Lane, made
obvious by the Church.

Places of Interest:
Little Moreton
Hall. (NT)

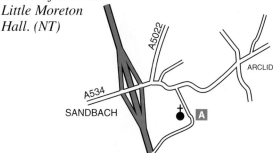

A The Chimney House Hotel,
Sandbach,
☎ 01270 764 141.

It was once the Rectory, but is now converted to
a modern hotel, with 48 bedrooms. It also has a
Conference Centre and Banqueting with
appropriate car parking and 8 acres of
woodland. There is outside seating. Children
but no dogs allowed. Morning coffee and
afternoon teas available.

Last orders:
 2 and 10pm,
but 9.30pm
on Sundays.

Price ££££

18 Middlewich Northwich Chester Holmes Chapel A54

No difficulty with this Exit.

Places of Interest: Capesthorne Hall. (HHA)

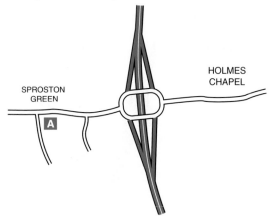

SPROSTON GREEN

HOLMES CHAPEL

A The Fox and Hounds.
Sproston Green,
☎ 01606 832 303

A wayside pub now owned by Pub Mistress. It has a restaurant and bars, with flagged floors and beamed ceilings. It has a Bowling Green, now out of use, and a beer garden. Children and dogs welcomed.

Last orders.
2.30 and 9pm,
but 8pm on
Sundays.
Closed
Monday night.

Price ££

to Carlisle

19 Northwich Altrincham A566
Knutsford A537 Holmes Chapel

The Exit itself is easy but busy, as the A556
feeds in from Cheshire. The Smoker at Plumley
may seem to be quite far.

Places of Interrest:
Arley Hall (HHA)
Tatton Park.(NT)
Tabley House.

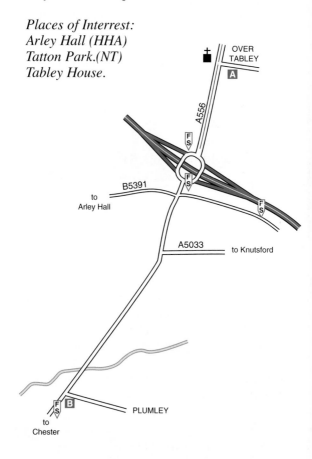

19 Continued

A The Old Vicarage.
Over Tabley.
☎ 01565 652 221.

A privately owned Residential Hotel with 5 double rooms. It has 2 acres of garden with a car park. Children must be over ten years old and dogs kept in cars. Log fires in the winter with home made soup to warm the extremities.

Last orders. 2.30pm
(for a light lunch)
and 9.30pm in the
evening for residents.

Price ££

B The Smoker.
Plumley
☎ 01565 722 338.

Named after a race horse bred by the Prince Regent, it is owned by Robinsons. A pleasant wayside pub which recently won the Chef of the Year Award. It prides itself on its Steak and Kidney Pie and the Pork de Tabley. It has a large garden, a comfortable restaurant, open fires and plenty of seating. The building is over 400 years old and is rumoured to have a ghost, so dogs not welcome.

Last orders.
2.15 and 9.30pm.
Sundays 9pm.

Price ££

to Carlisle

29 Preston Chorley A6 Blackburn

Not an easy Exit. Turn right at the traffic lights and bear right at the village green.

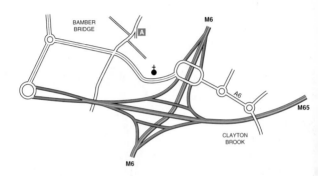

A Ye Olde Hob Inn,
Bamber Bridge,
☎ 01772 336 863.

A welcome surprise to find an old rustic, thatch roofed traditional pub, although it is owned by Scottish and Newcastle. It has a restaurant as well as a bar, with outside seating and a family room for wet weather. Children and coaches but no dogs.

Last orders.
2 and 9pm.
Closed on
Monday
evenings.

Price ££ *

Rugby

31 Preston Whalley A59 Clitheroe

Keep your head when negotiating the roundabouts on each side of the Motorway.

Places of Interest:
Samlesbury Hall.
(Samlesbury Hall Trust).

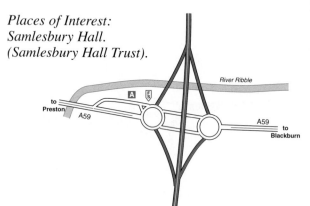

A The Tickled Trout Inn
Nr Samlesbury,
☎ 01772 877 671.

Now part of the Macdonalds hotel chain. It has 70 double and 2 single rooms; conference facilities; a leisure centre and a golf course nearby. For those who would merely like to sit looking at the river, there is outside seating. Children and dogs belonging to residents.

Last orders.
2 and 9.45pm.

Price ££££

to Carlisle

NORTHERN SECTION Junctions 33 - 44

This section is the most scenic of any of the motorways. From Junction 36 it begins to climb, with the Pennines on the right and the Lake District to the left. Penrith is a pleasant market town.

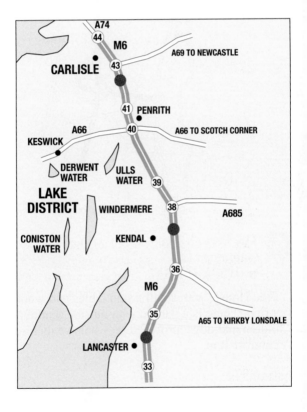

33 Lancaster Garstang A6 Fleetwood

Easy enough to get off the Motorway, but it should be treated as a comfort stop.

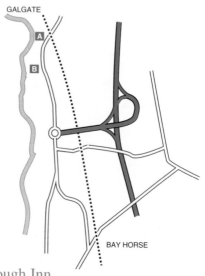

A The Plough Inn.
Galgate,
☎ 01524 751 337.

A Free House, with small round tables and wooden flooring. There is a garden with outside seating. Children and dogs, provided they behave themselves. A comfort stop.

Last orders.
2 and 8pm.

Price £

33 Continued

 Canalside Craft Centre,
Galgate.
☎ 01524 752 223.

An ideal spot for those just wanting a light
lunch and an airing for dogs or children along
the canal. Buffet style lunches only with home
made soups and cakes a speciality.

Last orders. 3pm on weekdays and
4pm on Saturdays and Sundays.

Price ££

35   Morecambe A6   Carnforth A601

Do not panic about the Motorway Interchange. The road to Over Kellet, which is an attractive village. still with its village shop, is easy to follow.

Places of Interest: Leighton Hall (HHA)

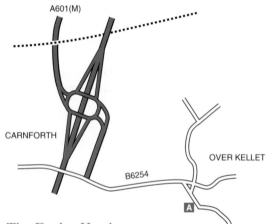

A601(M)

CARNFORTH

OVER KELLET

B6254

A

A   The Eagles Head.
Over Kellet.
☎ 01524 732 457.

A cheerful country pub owned by Mitchells. Bar meals served daily in a large dining area cum bar with exposed stone walls and timber ceilings. It specialises in home cured and cooked ham. It has a children's room, a beer garden and its own car park.

Last orders.
2 and 9pm
every day.

Price £

| 36 | South Lakes Kendal Barrow A590 Kirkby Lonsdale Skipton A65 Kendal Sedbergh A684 |

A boring Exit with dual carriageways on either side. Look out for the Crookland Hotel signs.

Places of Interest:
Levens Hall. (HHA)
Sizergh Castle.(NT)

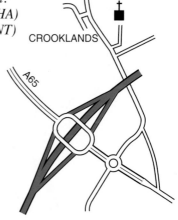

A Crooklands Hotel.
   Crooklands.
   ☎ 01539 567 432.

A privately owned hotel with 30 double rooms in a new extension. There is a restaurant and bars as well as a Carvery. Morning coffee and afternoon teas for the passing motorist. Children, but no dogs.

Last orders.
2 and 9pm
every day.

Price £££

38 Brough Kendal A685
Appleby B6260

Somewhat complicated with dual carriageways
leading off and onto the Motorway. After the
roundabout, drive through Tebay.

Places of Interest:
The Roman fort and
road at Low Borrowbridge.
(If you can get to it)

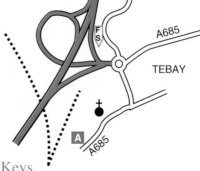

A The Cross Keys.
Tebay.
☎ 01539 624 240.

An old coaching inn on the way to Appleby. It is
privately owned with cheerful staff and still caters for
motorists with 6 double rooms(3 en suite) a beer
garden and the best Steak and Mushroom Pies in the
area. Children and dogs are
welcome, but dogs
to be controlled.

Last orders.
2.30 and 9pm
every day.

Price ££*

to Carlisle

39 Shap Kendal A6

An easy Exit.

Places of Interest: Shap Abbey. (EH)

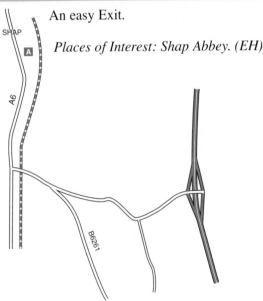

A The Greyhound Hotel,
Shap.
☎ 01931 716 474.

This must have been an elegant Georgian
coaching inn. It has however been modernised
to include copper topped tables in the bar. It has
2 bedrooms, but beware of the main railway line
just behind. A comfort stop.

Last orders. 2 and 9pm every day.

Price ££

40 North Lakes Keswick A66 Penrith Brough A68

A busy Exit with traffic coming in from the Lake District or going to Scotch Corner. Penrith was the crossing point for the coaching traffic going north and south, and also for those going to the Cumbrian ports, or else over the Pennines to Barnard Castle. As a result there is a plethora of old Coaching Inns and wayside pubs to this day.

The Red Rooster Roadstop, part of the Texaco garage at the first roundabout in Penrith does a good breakfast.

Places of Interest:
Dalemain. (HHA) Penrith Castle. The Toffee Shop. King Arthur's Round Table (EH). Mayburgh Henge (EH).

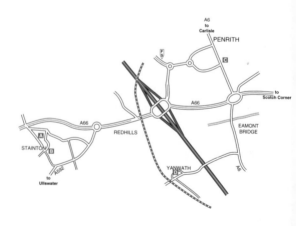

40 Continued

A The King's Arms.
Stainton.
☎ 01768 862 778.

A pub dating from 1721 in a rural Cumbrian village, it still serves home style cooking and a Steak and Kidney Pie made to an old recipe. It has a beer garden and serves bar meals. Dogs allowed but outdoors. The genial Scots host was a hotelier before becoming a ski instructor.

Last orders.
2 and 9pm in the summer. 8.30 in the winter.
Closed all day Monday from October to Easter.

B Brantwood Country Hotel
Stainton
☎ 01768 862 748

A family owned hotel and restaurant with 7 bedrooms and a large garden. An 18th century comfortably furnished house with oak beams and log fires.

Last food orders.
2.00 and 8.45pm everyday

Price ££

🛏

40 Continued

C The Yanwath Gate Inn
Yanwath
☎ 01768 862 386.

A privately owned pub dating from 1683. It is in a
quiet secluded backwater with a restaurant and bar,
as well as a beer garden. It specialises in fish dishes
and home cooking. Dogs and children allowed. The
sign over the door says "This gate hangs well and
hinders none. Refresh and pay and travel on".

Last orders.
2.15 to 9.30pm.
9pm on Sundays.

Price ££ *

 Continued

 The George Hotel
Penrith
☎ 01768 862 696.

A privately owned hotel in the centre of Penrith
which has been a Coaching Inn for the past 300
years, It is a fast disappearing example of old
style comfort, and has 23 double and 11 single
bedrooms. The carpark at the rear, where the
carriages used to be, is locked at nights.
Children are permitted and dogs at a charge.
There is no lift.

Last orders. 2.30 and 10pm.
9.30 on Sundays, during the winter.

Price £££

41 Wigton B5305

An easy Exit as the Stoneybeck is signed off the road. Those driving from the north might use this route if going to Penrith.

Places of Interest: Hutton in the Forest. (HHA)

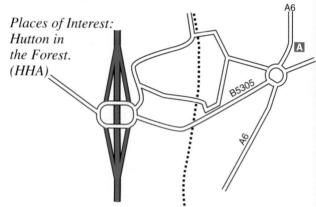

A Stoneybeck Inn.
Nr Penrith.
☎ 01768 862 369.

A Free House with standard furniture and wallpaper, which was once a coaching stop on the old A6. It has a restaurant and bars serving bar meals, including their speciality a Steak Pie. There is outside seating for warm days. A room inside for children and dogs allowed outside. A comfort stop.

Last orders 2.30
and 9pm every day.

Price ££

M6

43 Carlisle Brampton A69

Look out for the sign to Wetheral, which is about 5 minutes away. Also for the slip road into Warwick on Eden. The bridge over the Eden has traffic lights which can hold up traffic.

Places of Interest: Carlisle, with its Castle and early Norman Cathedral, (both much damaged by the Scots.) Wetheral Priory Gatehouse. Corby Castle.

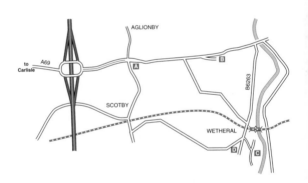

43 Continued

 The Waterloo.
Aglionby.
☎ 01228 513 347.

A small traditional wayside pub serving bar meals. It
has a beer garden and a car park at rear. Yes to
children, but no to dogs.

Last orders. 2.30pm
and 8.45 every day.

Price ££

 Queen's Arms Hotel.
Warwick on Eden.
☎ 01228 560 699.

The house itself is about 300 years old but was
converted into a pub in the 19th Century. It is a
pleasant and friendly place with a restaurant (where
wild salmon in Tarragon Sauce is a speciality) and a
bar as well as a lounge.
It also has 6 double bedrooms for the passing
traveller. Outside there is a beer garden and a
children's playground. Children allowed indoors but
dogs outside only.

Last orders.
1.45 and 8.45pm
every day.
Closed for
Monday lunches

Price ££

43 Continued

C The Crown Hotel.
Wetheral.
☎ 01228 561 888

An old Coaching Inn for the past 250 years but much enlarged and now part of the Shire Inns Group. It has a Leisure centre, banqueting and conference facilities, a sauna, swimming pool, etc. There are 47 double and 4 single bedrooms. Morning coffee and afternoon teas for those in a rush. Children and dogs permitted.

Last orders are
2 and 9.30pm.
(9pm om Sundays).

Price ££££

D The Fantails.
Wetheral
☎ 01228 560 239

A picturesque group of buildings overlooking the village green. It has a restaurant and a bar. There is a garden at the rear and car parking in front. Children but no dogs. A comfort stop.

Last orders.
2 and 9.30pm.
Closed all day
Mondays.

Price £££

44 **Carlisle**
Hawick A7 Brampton A689

The end of the M6 as a Motorway, but it continues as the dual carriageway A74, over the Border where it becomes the M74. To get back from the Wallfoot Hotel (which is just five minutes) you will have to retrace your way back to Junction 44.

Places of Interest: Hadrian's Wall.

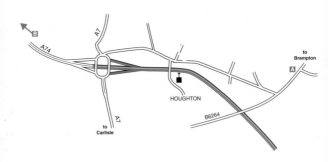

A Wallfoot Hotel.
Crosby on Eden.
☎ 01228 573 696.

A small privately owned hotel on the road between Brampton and the Motorway and close to the line of the turf section of Hadrian's Wall. It has 5 double and 2 single bedrooms. Home cooking is the order of the day. Dogs and children permitted in the garden at rear.

Last orders. 2 and 9pm every day, but no lunches on Mondays and Tuesdays.

Price £££

44 Continued

 B Metal Bridge Inn.
Blackford.
☎ 01228 674 044.

An old Coaching Inn, it is 4 miles beyond Exit 44 on the A74, on the banks of the River Esk, just before the Scottish Border. It is privately owned and in addition to a restaurant and bar it has 3 double and 2 single bedrooms. It prides itself on the Steak Pie which can be eaten outside when admiring the view over the river Esk to the Solway Firth and the mountains of Dumfriesshire. Children and dogs welcome, as are the many fisherman who come to stay here.

Last orders. 2 and 9pm every day.

Price ££

M10

Link to
St Albans

1 Abbots Langley A5183

This short 2 mile stretch was built in 1958 at the same time as the M1. With the opening of the M25, its usefulness declined so that now it is merely another way of getting onto the M1.
The only access point is from the A414. Take the road A5183 marked Park Street.

Places of interest;
St Albans Abbey.
Verulamium
Roman City
(EH).

CHISWELL GREEN

M 10

A414

A405

A

A The Swan
Abbots Langley
☎ 01923 672 539.

A typical pub offering bar meals and home cooking. Part of Greene King, it has recently been nominated as Pub of the Year from 158 others. Playground and outside seating.
Children but no dogs.
A comfort stop.

Last orders.
All day until
8.45pm.
(8pm on Sundays).

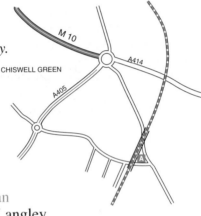

Price ££

London to Cambridge

It is a good alternative to the M1, for those travelling to or from the north and the Channel Tunnel, as it links up with the A1(M) at Huntingdon.

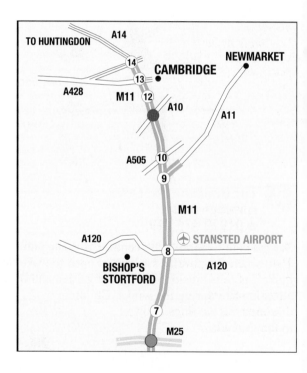

7 Harlow A414 Chelmsford

The roundabout is controlled by lights. Take the Chelmsford road and almost immediately turn off to the left on a small road which is marked St Clare Hospice and Hastingwood.

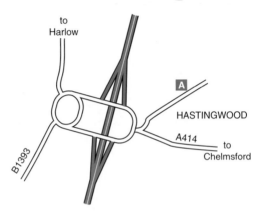

to
Harlow

A

HASTINGWOOD

A414
to
Chelmsford

B1393

A The Rainbow and Dove.
Hastingwood,
☎ 01279 415 419.

Said to date from the 15th century, it was a pub by 1640 when Cromwell's soldiers stopped to slake their thirst. There is outside seating in a garden and inside a roaring fire during the winter. Children discouraged, but dogs allowed in the grounds.

Last orders for food at 2.30pm and 9.30pm.

Price ££

to Cambridge

8 Stansted Airport
Bishop's Stortford A120

This Exit is being modernised to cope with the increasing traffic to and from Stansted Airport and construction work will continue for the forseable future. Keep going round the roundabout until you see the small turnoff for Birchanger.

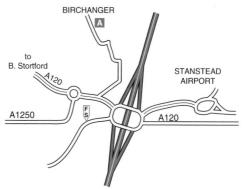

A The Three Willows.
Birchanger.
☎ 01279 815 913.

A quiet country pub with an interest in cricket, judging by the sign. Bar meals specialising in fish. Children's playground, where they are encouraged to stay outside. No dogs.

Last orders
2.30pm
and 9.30pm.
No evening
meals on
Sundays.

Price £££

9 Newmarket A11 Norwich (Restricted access)

This junction gives direct access to the Newmarket road. Turn off where marked Great Chesterford before crossing over the road. If driving north, you must access again at Junction 10 and vice versa.

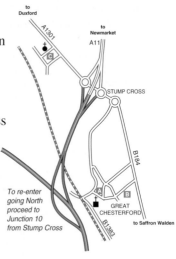

Places of interest: Audley End (EH), Saffron Walden

 The Crown House Hotel
Great Chesterford.
☎ 01799 530 515.

There has been a building on the site since Roman times. The foundations of the present one date from 1560. It is privately owned hotel with modern stone flagged floors and 22 bedrooms. The chef bakes his own bread; cures his own fish and meat and prepares the pastas.

Last orders for meals 9.00pm including Sundays.
Dogs, children and the disabled are provided for.

Price £££

to Cambridge

9 Continued

The Plough.
Great Chesterford.
☎ 01799 530 283.

A village pub for 200 years and owned by
Greene King. It has a modern restaurant and
bar. Large children's playground and family
room. Outside seating where children and dogs
are welcome.

Last orders for meals
are 2.20 and 9.00pm.
No food on
Sunday evenings.

Price ££

The Red Lion.
Hinxton.
☎ 01799 530 601.

A 16th century pub but brought up to more
modern standards in this attractive village.
Home cooking in the restaurant and bar. The
yellow headed Amazon parrot is semi-retired,
but a black cat - Charlie, entertains the guests
as well as a stuffed tarantula. Dogs and children
permitted in the garden but no coaches.

Last orders are
1.45 and 9.45pm
including Sundays.

Price £££

M11

London

10 Royston A505 Newmarket A11 Saffron Walden

An easy enough Exit, but it could get congested when there is a flying display at the Imperial War Museum.
Exit here if you are driving South to go to Great Chesterford or Saffron Walden.

Places of interest:
The Imperial
War Museum
and American
Air Museum.

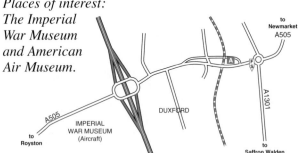

A The Red Lion Hotel,
Whittlesford.
☎ 01223 832 047.

An old black and white half timbered house, now a hotel, with a chapel open to the public. It is privately owned with a restaurant and bars. There are 17 bedrooms and a garden. Breakfasts for the passer-by. Children and dogs are allowed.

Last orders
for meals are
2.30 and
9.00pm.

Price ££

12 Cambridge A603 Sandy

Do not be too put off by the modern
development into Barton. The picturesque
village of Grantchester, made famous by the
First World War poet Rupert Brooke, ("-honey
still for tea.")
is easy to find.

Places of interest:
Wimpole Hall (NT)

to Cambridge

A603

BARTON

B

GRANTCHESTER

A

C

F
S

A The Green Man,
Grantchester.
☎ 01223 841 178.

A traditional village pub with wooden floors. It
has a restaurant and bar. Extensive car park at
the rear. Children and dogs allowed in the
garden. Afternoon teas, honey extra.

Last orders;
3 and 9pm.

Price ££

12 Continued

B The Rupert Brooke
Grantchester.
☎ 01223 840 295.

Converted from a 19th century house, it is now a folksy, but cheerful pub, complete with beams. There is outside seating at the front.
Children, but no dogs or coaches.

Last orders;
2 and 9pm.

Price £££

C The White Horse
Barton
☎ 01223 262 327.

A popular pub, owned by Greene King, which has recently been extended. It has a restaurant, carvery and a Bar, as well as five bedrooms. Outside there is a children's playground, a beer garden and a car park.
Children and dogs, but outside.

Last orders;
2 and 9.30pm.

Price ££

to Cambridge

13/14 Cambridge A1303
Bedford A428

Exit 13 is easy for those coming from the
South, but Exit 14, for those from the North,
will require a Degree in map reading. However
well worth the effort to get to Madingley.

Places of interest:
Madingley Hall.
American
Military
Cemetery

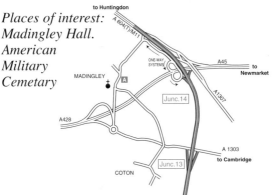

A The Three Horseshoes.
Madingley.
☎ 01954 210 221.

Part of a chain of well managed Restaurants
cum Pubs, it is comfortable and smart. Inside
there is a restaurant and long bar, with a
conservatory at the rear. Outside there is a beer
garden in a pleasant garden. A comfortable stop
over.

Last orders are 2pm
and 9pm. On Sunday
evenings Bar Grills
are available.

Price ££££*

M18

M1 Rotherham

Junctions **1** to **6**

This 30 mile Motorway was built to link the M1 to the A1(M) at Doncaster, then with the M180 spur to Grimsby and finally with the M62 Trans Pennine near Goole. It is a useful linking motorway, as one can switch from the M1 or else cut off a corner when travelling from or to Hull.

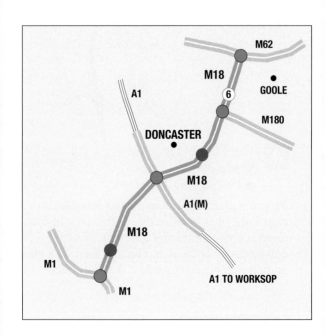

to Goole

6 Thorne A614

This is an area of low fen land and irrigation ditches. The Waterside, where canal boats once disgorged their cargoes, was renowned for having seven pubs, but only one now remains. It is said that an Elizabethan warship was built here to harass the Armada.

Places of interest;
The birthplace of Thomas Crapper, the manufacturer of flushing lavatories.

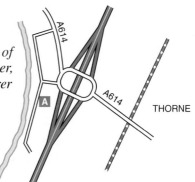

A The John Bull Inn.
Waterside.
☎ 01405 814 677.

A comfortable inn, by the canal, where ale has been served to thirsty bargemen since the 1500s. It has a restaurant which is used in the evening and otherwise serves bar meals. Children and dogs are welcome.

Last orders. 2.30 and 9.30pm every day.

Price ££

M20

London

Junctions **1** to **13**

The M20 is 40 miles long and was started in 1961 and finished twenty years later. It is the main Motorway from the Channel Ports to link up directly with the Motorway system and to circumnavigate London to get to the North and West.

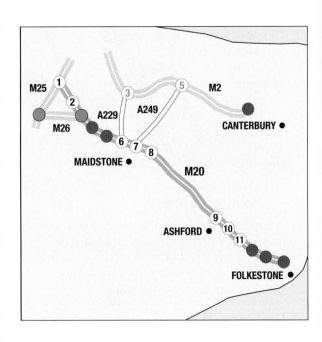

 Junction with Exit 3 of the M25

It is not so complicated as it may appear. Follow the signs to Farningham and do not be put off by passing the Highways Recycling Centre. Turn right at the roundabout by the Fina Station. It is still a surprisingly attractive rural village although so near to London.

Attractions: Eynsford Castle.(EH)
Lullingstone Roman Villa (EH).

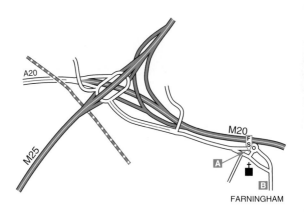

129

1 Continued

A The Chequers.
Farningham.
☎ 01322 865 222.

An honest to goodness local pub serving bar meals at lunch only with home made pies, sandwiches and a range of beers and stout. Some seating outside on the pavement and dogs are welcome.
Street parking only.

Last orders
2.30pm.

Price £

B Pied Bull.
Farningham
☎ 01322 862 125

It was known as The Bull in 1612 and two hundred years later six coaches a day used to stop here. It has recently been refurbished and produces bar meals, especially their Steak and Kidney Pie. Dogs and children under control welcomed in the enclosed garden.

Last food orders
2.00 and 8.45pm
No evening meals
on Sunday.
Closed Mondays.

Price ££

2 Paddock Wood Gravesend Tonbridge (A22)

Exit 2 is in reality two exits joined by a normal road! Coming from London it is easy enough to get off at the first Exit to get to the Bull Hotel in Wrotham, which is a picturesque village, but you must then rejoin by driving to Exit 2a on the M26 which joins the M20 a mile further on! It is not as bad as it sounds. The converse is true for those driving from the East.

Places of interest: Brands Hatch Racing Circuit.

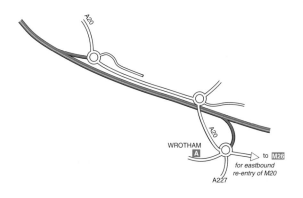

2 Continued

A Bull Hotel
Wrotham
☎ 01732 789 800.

A family run hotel in a building which is a Listed
Georgian house, but the interior has been done over
to give an open plan appearance. It has a restaurant
and a bar. Morning Coffee for the passer by. For the
overnight guests, there are 2 single and 10 double
bedrooms. Wrotham itself is a picturesque village .
A comfort stop.

Last orders. 2 and 9.45pm (9.30pm on Sundays).

Price £££

6 Maidstone Chatham A229

There have been road improvements to the A229 which has made it easier to reach the two places mentioned.

Places of interest:
Kits Coty,
prehistoric burial
mound
Museum of Kent life.

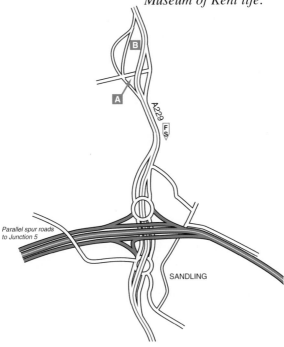

6 Continued

A Lower Bell.
Blue Bell Hill
☎ 01634 861 127.

The word Lower in the name is appropriate as it is now surrounded by high embankments of the new road layout. That does not detract from the warm welcome and home cooking and choice of four Real Ales on offer.
There is some outside seating at the rear where dogs are allowed.

Last orders.
2.45 and 9.45pm
every day.

Price ££

B Kits Coty Restaurant & Brasserie
Kits Coty.
☎ 01634 684 445.

A family run restaurant for the past 16 years, it has a sweeping view over Maidstone and the Weald. A well kept garden enhances its surroundings. Modern art deco furnishing with glass and chrome.

Last orders.
2 and 10pm but
closed for
Saturday lunch
and on Mondays.

Price ££

 **Maidstone Sheerness
Canterbury Ramsgate A249**

This Exit is close to Maidstone and therefore it is a more built up area. The new Eurostar railtrack makes it more confusing.

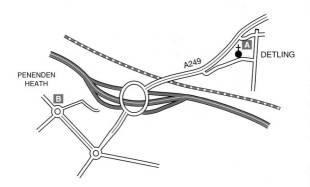

 The Cock Horse.
Detling.
☎ 01622 737 092.

A local pub in the middle of this rural village, although hemmed in by new roads. It has a beamed restaurant and bar, where imaginative home cooking is served and coffee all day. A secluded garden at the rear where dogs and children are welcome.

Last orders.
From 11am to
10.30pm every day.

Price ££

7 Continued

B The Chiltern Hundreds
Penenden Heath.
☎ 01622 752 335.

It has been a coaching stop since 1830, but why it
should give the impression of giving an MP the
chance to leave Parliament in a hurry is not known.
It is now part of the Chef and Brewer chain, so is
now in the form of open areas serving bar meals
from 11.00 in the morning. Some outside seating and
a large carpark. Facilities for the disabled but dogs
not welcome. A comfort stop.

Last orders. 10pm.
(9.30pm on Sundays).

Price £££

8 Lenham A20

Not a complicated Exit, but look out for the sign
to Hollingbourne.

Places of interest: Leeds Castle. (HHA)
Stoneacre. (NT)

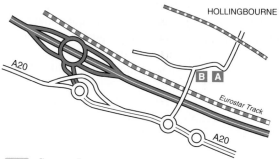

HOLLINGBOURNE

A20

B A

Eurostar Track

A20

A Sugar Loaves.
Hollingbourne.
☎ 01622 880 220.

Dating from 1740, it is now a village pub. It has
a beer garden and its own car park. Bar meals
are served and dogs are welcome. A pool table
for wet days.

Last orders. 2 and 9pm
every day.

Price ££

8 Continued

B The Windmill
Hollingbourne.
☎ 01622 880 280.

A privately owned pub, which dates back in parts to
the 16th Century, in this attractive village.
It has a restaurant and bar with home cooked meals.
Outside there is a new playground and a beer garden
at the rear, with seating in front.
Dogs welcome provided the owners make them
behave.

Last orders. 2.30 and 10pm.
(9.30pm on Saturdays and Sundays).

Price ££

to Folkestone

9 **Ashford A20**
Canterbury A28

A modern Exit and road system, which does not seem to bode well in finding a suitable pub, but persist.

Places of interest: Godington Park.

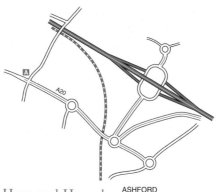

ASHFORD

A Hare and Hounds.
Potters Corner.
☎ 01233 621 760.

Once an 18th century inn, it has been thoroughly modernised, but still retains its character and serves real ales. The road outside is busy, but there is some outside seating. It is well known for its food and wines.

Last orders.
2.30 and
9.30pm.
Closed
Monday
evenings.

Price ££

10   Ashford A292

A built up area, not helped by a large Tesco just off
the Motorway. The pubs are pleasant enough when
you reach them, but you may prefer to treat it
as a comfort stop.

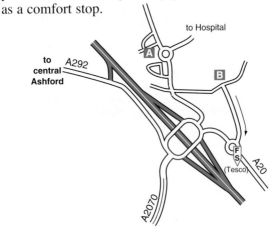

A   White Horse.
Willesborough Lees.
☎ 01233 624 257.

Built about 1840, it is not known whether it has
always been a pub. Today it gives a friendly
welcome to the motorist, where bar meals are
available with home cooking and morning coffee.
There is a secluded garden at rear, but dogs are not
welcome. A pool table
for wet weather.

Last orders.
2.30 and 9.30pm.
Closed Sunday and
Monday evenings.

Price ££

10 Continued

B Blacksmiths Arms
Willesborough Green.
☎ 01233 623 975.

Some 300 years old, and probably the site of the
smithy, the forge is now replaced by log fires,
and the heat reduced by pints of Real Ale, in
either the beamed restaurant or the bar where
home cooked food is served.
There is a large garden at the rear where dogs
are welcome. One armed bandits for the bored.

Last orders. 2.30 and 9.00pm. 9pm on
Sundays).

Price ££

11 Canterbury B 2068
Hastings A259 Hythe A261

The new Eurostar track now runs alongside the
Motorway. Circle round to the north on the B 2068
and the pub can be seen on the left.

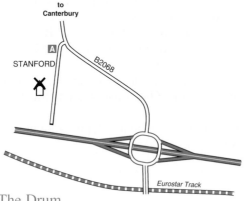

to
Canterbury

A

STANFORD

B2068

Eurostar Track

A The Drum
Stanford
☎ 01303 812 125.

It is the last pub (or first) before the tunnel. It has
been a country pub for some 200 years. Log fires still
burn in the grates. The present landlord has been
there for 34 years and will give you a friendly
welcome. There is a restaurant and a bar for snacks
and Real Ales. Outside seating in the garden. Dogs
welcome. Sunday Roasts
are their
speciality.

Last orders.
2.30 and 9pm
every day.

Price ££

Junctions 7 to 11

Built to give quick access from Gatwick Airport to London, this 18 mile stretch took nearly four years to complete.

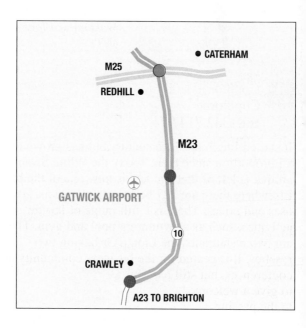

10 Crawley
East Grinstead A264

An easy Exit and the Hotel is on the other side of the roundabout.

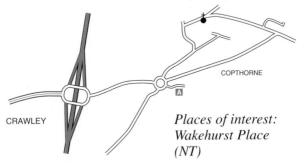

COPTHORNE

CRAWLEY

Places of interest:
Wakehurst Place
(NT)

A Copthorne Hotel
Copthorne
☎ 01342 714 971.

It started life in the 16th century,but has grown out of all proportion since then. Today the White Swan is all that is left of that age and is now one of the bars. Elsewhere there are 227 bedrooms of various sizes, uses and prices. There is a full range of leisure activities, such as a swimming pool and gym. There are two restaurants, the Lion d'Or having two rosettes. It is geared for the business community and conferences, but still has time
to give a welcome
to the passing
motorist.

Last orders,
2 and 10.45pm.

Price ££££

London Orbital

Junctions **4** to **26**

The idea of an orbital ring road round London was first mooted in 1905 with a 12 mile radius. Concentric bypasses were tried which failed, so in 1975, a decision was made to construct an integrated Orbital Ring Road which would give access to the West and the North via the Dartford Crossing from the Channel Ports; as well as give a direct connection between Heathrow and Gatwick and be a conduit for the Motorways leading into London. The entire Orbital Motorway was finished in 1986.

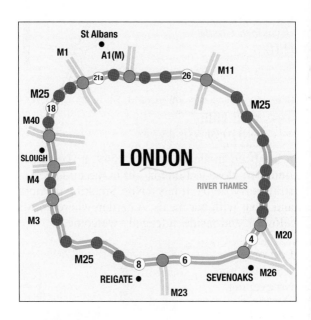

4 Bromley A21
Orpington A224

As an exit, it is an easy one, but at the roundabout look out for a narrow lane signed Well Hill.

Places of interest: Lullingstone Roman VIlla (EH) Lullingstone Castle(HHA) Eynsford Castle (EH).

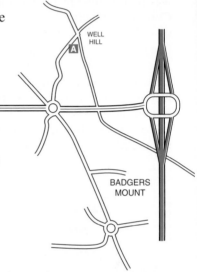

A Bo Peep Restaurant.
Well Hill.
☎ 01959 534 457.

It has been an alehouse since 1549. It is a surprise to find it so close to London, set in the middle of strawberry fields. It has a Non Smoking restaurant and a bar with bar meals. A garden where dogs are allowed, and inside, a friendly welcome.

Last orders
2 and 9.45pm.
No evening
meals on
Sundays.

Price ££ *

Orbital

M25

6 Westerham Eastbourne
Caterham Godstone A22

This should not be any
trouble but do not take
the dual carriageway.
Godstone is an
attractive place,
surrounding a
village green.

Places of interest:
Chartwell (NT)
Squerryes Court
(HHA) Quebec House.

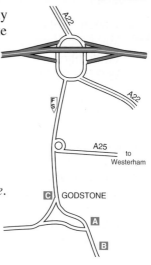

A The White Hart.
Godstone.
☎ 01883 742 521.

Said to have been established in the reign of
Richard II and enlarged in the time of good
Queen Bess. It is now part of the Beefeater
chain and therefore somewhat formalised.
It is still a cheerful place with original beams,
log fires and efficient service.
There is outside
seating and a
car park.

Last orders.
2.30 and 10.30 pm
(9pm on Sundays).

Price ££

6 Continued

B Coach House Restaurant
and Godstone Hotel.
Godstone.
☎ 01883 742 461.

A family run hotel, it is a comfortable friendly place.
It is some 400 years old, but not as old as the willow
tree in the garden. For those wishing to stay, after
tasting one of their flambéed specialities at dinner in
the Coach House Restaurant, there are 8 double
bedrooms available.
Dogs are welcome but outdoors.

Last orders. 2 and 10pm. (9pm on Sundays)
Closed all day Mondays.

Price £££

6 Continued

C The Hare and Hounds
Godstone
☎ 01883 742 296.

A traditional English village pub, with beamed eating areas. There is some outside seating under a spreading chestnut tree. Children and dogs are not encouraged, but the welcome inside is more than encouraging.

Last orders. 3 and 9.30pm. Sundays, all day until 9pm.

Price ££

8 Sutton Reigate A217

Keep a look-out after the roundabout as you might easily miss the turning. If you do, carry on to the crossroads.

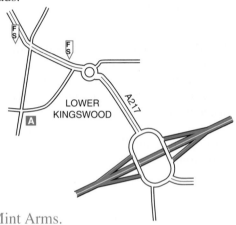

A Mint Arms.
Lower Kingswood.
☎ 01737 242 957.

A Free House pub tucked away in a small village. It does have a restaurant as well as the usual bars where bar meals are available. Outside there is a playground, a beer garden where they have Barbeques, weather permitting and dogs and children are allowed. A pool table and dart board for wet days.

Last orders.
3 and 10pm.
(9.30pm on Sundays).

Price £££

Orbital

M25

18 Rickmansworth Chorleywood
Amersham A404

An easy Exit but at the cross roads look out for
Dog Kennel Road.

Places of interest:
Chenies Manor
House.

CHORLEYWOOD

A404

A

RICKMANSWORTH

A The Black Horse.
Chorleywood Common.
☎ 01923 282 252.

This could be deep in the countryside instead of
being just off the Motorway. It has been a pub
since the early 1800s and still produces home
cooked specials. There is seating at the front
and a beer garden at the rear. Children are
welcome, and dogs can stretch their legs on the
Common.

Last orders.
2.15 and 9.15pm.

Price £££ *

21a St Albans A405

This looks a a complicated Exit, but you just follow the signs.

Places of interest:
St Albans
Abbey.
Verulanium
Roman
City.

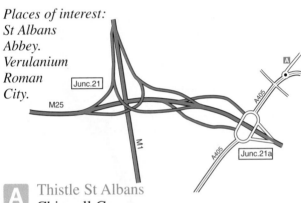

A Thistle St Albans
Chiswell Green
☎ 01727 854 252.

This hotel is not for the casual passer-by, as it sets a high standard in comfort and price. There are 111 bedrooms to suit every wish and supported by every form of comfort and relaxation, such as a swimming pool, gym and a sauna. There is a restaurant, carvery and bars. Morning coffee and afternoon teas are also served to those wanting to pause. Children and dogs are welcomed.

Last orders.
2 and 9.30pm.
(9pm on Sundays)

Price ££££

26 Waltham Abbey Loughton A121

You should not get lost on this Exit, but treat both as a comfort stop.

Places of interest: Waltham Abbey, Gatehouse and Bridge (EH). Epping Forest.

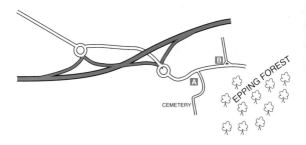

A The Volunteer,
Nr Waltham Abbey.
☎ 01992 713 705.

A McMullens pub which has recently been modernised. It specialises in Chinese food. You can have the usual bar meals in the bar. No children, and dogs stay outside. A comfort stop.

Last orders.
10.00pm
(8.30pm
on Sundays).

Price £££

26 Continued

 The Woodbine
Nr Waltham Abbey.
☎ 01992 713 050.

A typical locals' pub but with a non-smoking
Conservatory serving bar meals. You can
contemplate the edge of Epping Forest. A comfort
stop.

Last orders. 3 and 9pm.
4pm on Sundays.

Price £

M20/M25 Link

2a Borough Green
Maidstone A25

An 8 mile stretch of Motorway, built in 1980, to form the southern link of the M20 with the M25.

A useful Exit for those who have misread the M20 signs and find themselves on the M26 going west, as they can rejoin the M20 at Wrotham.

*Places of interest: Old Soar Manor (EH)
Ightam Mote. (NT) St Leonards Tower. (EH)*

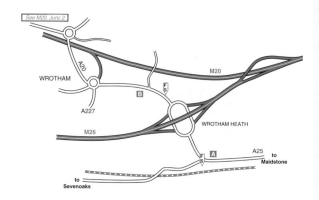

2a Continued

A The Vineyard.
Wrotham Heath.
☎ 01732 882 330.

A family run restaurant, specialising in sea food and French and Italian cooking. Although on the road, it is surrounded by a secluded garden and private car park. Small and friendly. Childen allowed but no dogs.

Last orders.
2.30 and 10.30pm.

Price £££

B The Moat.
Wrotham Green.
☎ 01732 882 263.

Although part of the Beefeater chain, it still retains a traditional atmosphere, with its beams and old fashioned charm. There is some outside seating, where you can have bar meals, if you do not want to use the restaurant.
Children but no dogs.

Last orders.
All day to 10pm.
(9pm on Sundays)
Sunday evenings.

Price ££

Junctions **1** to **12**

The M27, 27 miles long, was built to connect Portsmouth and Southampton with the M3. It ends rather abruptly at the edge of the New Forest, but continues as a dual carriageway nearly as far as Bournemouth.

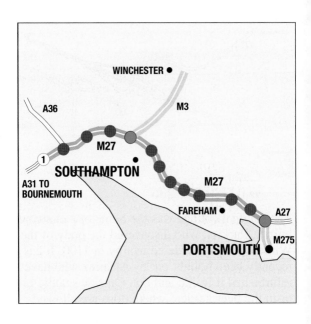

M27   **New Forest**

1   Lyndhurst
     Cadnam A337

Once off the Exit, you might miss the sign to the Sir John Barleycorn. On the other side of the junction, the road will take you into the New Forest proper, but you will not get lost.

Places of interest: The Rufus Stone. Hamptworth Lodge (HHA) Paulton's Park. Broadlands House (HHA)
Newhouse, Redlynch.(HHA)

A   Sir John Barleycorn
     Cadnam
     ☎ 02380 812 236.

The original cottage was the home of a charcoal burner, Purkiss, who discovered the body of the King William Rufus murdered nearby in 1100. It has recently been bought out by Alcatraz who have refurbished it inside and out. Outside seating in front or in the beer garden, where dogs are allowed.

Last orders. 9.30pm
(9pm on Sundays).

Price ££

 Continued

 The White Hart.
Cadnam
☎ 02380 812 277.

A Coaching Inn since the 17th century, it still gives warm hospitality, with log fires and a profusion of hanging baskets. Home cooking specialising in fish. There is a playground and a secluded garden where dogs are allowed.

Last orders.
2 and 9.30pm
(9pm on Sundays).

Price £££ *

 The Bell Inn
Brook
☎ 02380 812 214.

A family run hotel, which is really a comfortable annex to the Bramshaw Golf Club in the vicinity. It has been an Inn for at least 200 years and has 2 single and 23 double rooms, as well as a restaurant, bars, playground, family room, beer garden and outside seating. For the casual visitor there is morning coffee or afternoon tea. Non golfers are also welcome!

Last orders.
2.30 and 9.30pm.

Price £££

 Continued

 The Green Dragon.
Brook
☎ 02380 813 359.

A Whitbred owned pub, it has been a Beerhouse for
200 years, before which it was used by a coffin
maker and before him by a Wheelwright. No sign of
the coffin maker is now apparent, only a friendly,
cheerful atmosphere, in the bar and beamed areas for
eating.

Last orders. 2 and 9.30pm (9pm on Sundays).

Price £££

London to Birmingham

Junctions **2** to **16**

The M40 was completed to take the pressure off the M1. This it suceeded in doing to such an extent that now it is almost as crowded as the M1 itself. However it is an alternative route to vary the scenery.

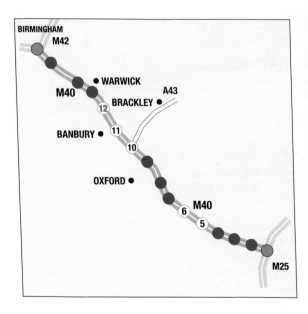

5 Stokenchurch West Wycombe A40

Easy enough to find Stokenchurch.
Places of interest: West Wycombe Park (NT)
The Hell Fire Club.
Hughenden Manor (NT)

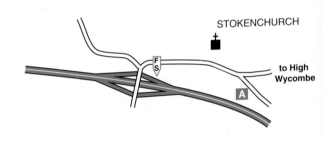

A Ye Fleur de Lys.
Stokenchurch.
☎ 01494 482 269.

A village pub on the green. Built in 1886, judging by the date on the building, it is an unassuming local pub, but with beams and an open fire. Children's playground and a beer garden, in which dogs are allowed. A comfort stop.

Last orders. 2.30 and 10.30pm (10pm on Sundays).

Price ££

to Birmingham

6 Watlington Thame
Princes Risborough B4009

The road to Lewknor can be easily missed, so
look out for the sign on the right. The village
itself is attractive.

A Ye Olde Leather Bottel
Lewknor
☎ 01844 351 482.

Ye Olde Leather Bottel is 450 years old, which
makes for a congenial atmosphere. It specialises
in home cooking and serves morning coffee as
well as Brakspears traditional ales. There is
plenty of outside seating in a large garden.
Childrens playground and facilities for the
disabled. Dogs welcome.

Last orders.
2 and 9.30pm
every day.

Price £££ *

10 Northampton A43

A simple Exit off the Motorway on to the old road
between Oxford and Brackley.

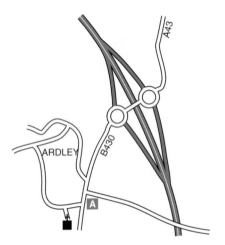

A Fox and Hounds
Ardley
☎ 01869 346 883

Now owned by an ex-submariner, this 18th Century
pub on the old coaching road, serves morning coffee
to the passing motorist as well as bar meals. A beer
garden at the rear and its own car parking. Dogs are
welcome, as are ex-servicemen
who served near by.

Last orders.
2.30 and 9.30pm.
Closed on
Sunday evenings.

Price ££

11 Banbury A422

The main exit for Banbury. Take the road towards Brackley, but turn right after about 100 yards signed Nethercote and Overthorpe. Do not be put off by the narrow lane. An alternative is to come in from Banbury, but that is more complicated.

A The Bowling Green
Overthorpe
☎ 01295 265 465

The drawback to this pub is that it is next to the Motorway. However its friendliness will soon dispel the noise. Interesting menu as it specialises in home made sausages and Thai food. Outside seating and car park. A comfort stop.

Last orders.
2 and 9.30pm
every day.

Price ££

M40 London to Birmingham

12 Gaydon B4451

Turn left when you get to the A41 and the pub will be on your right hand side.

Places of interest:
Heritage Motor
Museum
Edgehill Battlefield. 1642
Upton House (NT).

A The Gaydon Inn
Gaydon
☎ 01926 640 388

An brick coloured building by the side of the road, which specialises in Beef and Ale Pie. It will also give morning coffee to the thirsty motorist. A childrens playground and a beer garden. Dogs allowed.
A comfort stop.

Last orders.
2.30 and 9.30pm
(9pm Sundays).

Price ££

Junctions **1** to **11**

Completed in 1986, it is still to be continued as
a Motorway to join up with the M1 at
Nottingham. It is in effect the southern part of
the Birmingham Ring Road, with the M6 and
the M5 completing the circuit. It is a useful
linkage for those using the M40 from and to the
North.

M42 — Bromsgrove

3 Birmingham Redditch
Evesham A435

Take the slip road towards Portway – over the dual carriageway and back towards the restaurant.

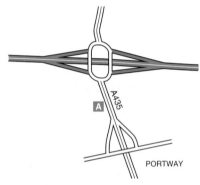

A Portway Italian Restaurant
Portway
☎ 01564 824 794

An Italian restaurant specialising in Italian dishes. A comfortable small restaurant. No dogs.

Last food orders.
2.30 and 10.30pm.
No evening meals
on Sunday.
Closed Monday.

Price ££

9 Coventry (N&E) A446

No great difficulties to find the place.

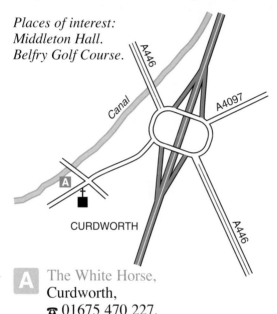

Places of interest:
Middleton Hall.
Belfry Golf Course.

A446

Canal

A4097

A446

 CURDWORTH

A The White Horse,
Curdworth,
☎ 01675 470 227.

Now owned by Vintage Inns it is still a pleasant
folksy place with coal fires in the winter. There
is outside seating where dogs are allowed as
well as children. Bar meals served as there is no
restaurant as such.

Last orders
10pm every day.

Price ££

11 Burton on Trent
Nuneaton A444

A twisty road system to
reach Appleby Magna,
but not impossible.
Keep the church
in view.

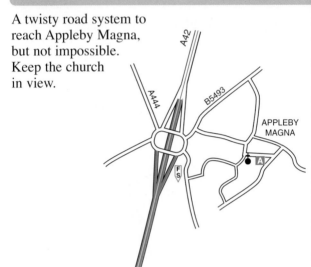

A The Black Horse,
Appleby Magna,
☎ 01530 270 588.

An old 16th or 17th Century building. It is a simple
village pub owned by Marstons. It serves bar meals
and has some outside seating as well as a family
room. Dogs are welcome.

Last orders. 9.30pm.
No lunches on weekdays
Bar lunch on Sundays
but no evening meal.

Price £

1 Avonmouth A403

This used to be the last Exit on the M4 before crossing over into Wales. With the building of another bridge over the Severn, this section was renamed M48 and the new section became the M4, for some illogical reason.

Places of interest: St Augustine's Vineyard

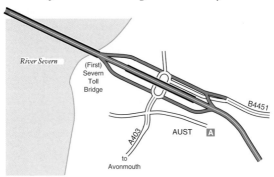

A Boars Head.
Aust
☎ 01454 632 278.

A late 18th Century village pub, which probably was a coaching stop for those crossing over to Wales on the ferry. It gives a friendly welcome to all, enhanced in winter by log fires and home made cooking. There is a beer garden where dogs are welcome.

Last orders.
2.15 and 9.15pm.
No evening meals
on Sundays.

Price £££

2 Chepstow A48

Chepstow is just off the Exit and is well worth a visit, especially the castle. There are other restaurants, hotels and pubs in the town.

Places of interest:
Tintern Abbey. (EH)
Caerwent
(Roman Silures)
Offa's Dyke.
Chepstow Castle. (EH)

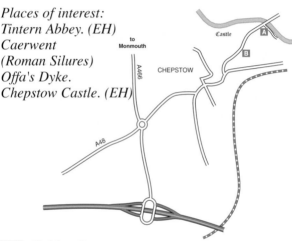

A Bridge Inn
Chepstow.
☎ 01291 625 622,

Said to be the oldest pub in Chepstow, being the first or last in Wales, on the bridge over the River Wye. It is a cheerful old fashioned place with a restaurant upstairs and a bar. Outside there is a beer garden and a private car park.
Children and dogs are welcome.

Last orders.
2.30 and 9pm every day.

Price £

2 **Continued**

 B Castle View Hotel.
Chepstow
☎ 01291 620 349.

As the name implies, it really does have a view
up to the castle. Some 350 years old, it has been
modernised to provide 2 single and 11 double
bedrooms, mostly in external annexes. Outside
there is a beer garden at the rear, whilst indoors
there is a restaurant and a bar. There are
facilities for the disabled and children and dogs
are welcome. It has recently changed hands.

Last orders.
2 and 9.30pm.
Residents only
for Sunday evening.

Price £££

CASTLE VIEW HOTEL, CHEPSTOW.

Junctions **1** to **4**

The M 50 was one of the first Motorways to be built and for some years,was in splendid isolation until joined to the M 5. It was built to connect the Midlands with South Wales but only goes as far as Ross on Wye before continuing as dual-carriageway to Newport, passing through or near some historic towns such as Monmouth and Raglan. It is also a way of driving to Wales without paying the Toll charges levied on the Severn Bridges!

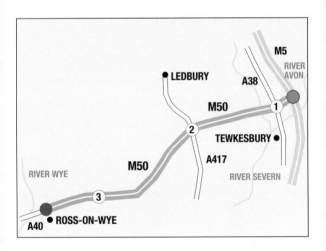

 Malvern Tewkesbury A38

A relatively easy Exit. Just follow the signs to Twyning. The Fleet Inn is brown signed from the roundabout.

Places of interest. Tewkesbury Abbey.

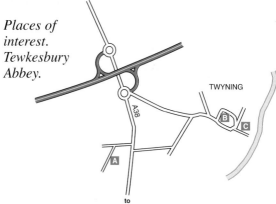

A Puckrup Hall Hotel
Puckrup
☎ 01684 296 200.

An ex-Stakis hotel, now owned by Hiltons with all the trimmings including an 18 hole Championship Golf Course: two restaurants and bars; Leisure Centre and swimming pool. 112 bedrooms (16 in the original building) and meals until 2pm and 10pm. A comfortable base for those exploring the area.

Price ££££

Continued

B The Village Inn
Twyning
☎ 01684 293 500.

Overlooking the village green it was once a bakery,
then a shop and Post office and is now a friendly old
fashioned pub.

Last orders are
2.30 and 11.00pm.
Closed Monday
and Tuesday lunch.

Price £

C The Fleet Inn
Twyning
☎ 01684 274 310.

By the side of the River Avon, it is a popular place,
with some bedrooms. An open area for bar meals and
outside seating on a terrace by the banks of the river.
Dogs allowed on leads.

Last orders for dinner
in the restaurant
is 9.00pm.

Price ££

2 Gloucester A417
Hereford Ledbury 417

Take the road to Gloucester to find the Rose
and Crown which is about a mile from the Exit.

*Places of interest. Eastnor Castle. (HHA).
Ledbury.*

PLAYLEY
GREEN

A

to
Staunton

A The Rose and Crown
Redmarly D'Abitot
☎ 01531 650 234.

An wayside pub owned by Pubmaster, dating
from the 1800s with the addition of a later
Assembly Room which is now the restaurant.
No evening meals on Sunday. Outside seating.
Dogs and children allowed. A comfort stop.

Last orders
for food are
2pm and9.15pm
No evening
meals on
Sunday.

Price ££

M50

**M5 to
Ross on Wye**

3 Gwent B4211

The only T junction exit in the U.K which is known
in the trade as a Compact Grade Separation! Take the
road to Kilcot.

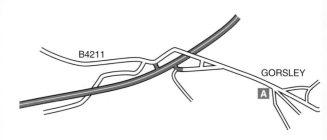

B4211

GORSLEY

A

A The Roadmaker Inn
Gorsley
☎ 01989 720 352.

A Free House, specialising in local beef and
vegetables. Children but no dogs. Outside seating
and a congenial atmosphere as it has been a pub
since 1840.

Last orders
2 and 9pm
No food on
Sunday &
Monday
Night.

Price ££

Birkenhead to Chester

Junctions **1** to **12**

A short 12 mile stretch of Motorway passing through the densely industrialised area of Ellesmere Port. The Wirral however still has rural charm.

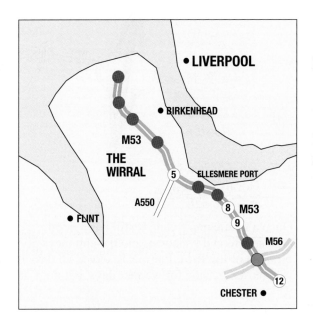

5 Queensferry A41
Birkenhead

Turn left at the traffic lights to reach the car park.

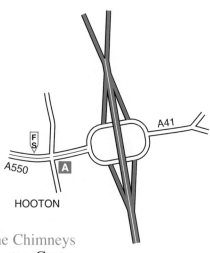

HOOTON

A The Chimneys
Hooton Green,
☎ 0151 326 2820

Once a gentlemen's club, it still has a good
atmosphere and welcome, and the chimneys give
promise of log fires. Bar meals served all day. There
is a garden outside for warmer days, but dogs are no
welcome.

Last food
orders. 10pm
9pm Sundays.

Price ££

to Chester

 Ellesmere Port
Boat Museum A50532

Just follow the signs to the Boat Museum.

Places of interest: The Boat Museum.

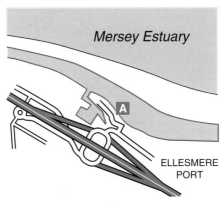

A Rotate Restaurant
Ellesmere Port,
☎ 01513 555 017

The restaurant specialises in contemporary mediterranean cuisine for light lunches.

Last food orders.
9.30pm.

Price £

12 Chester A51

There is danger of continuing past the junction on the dual carriageway A55 to Wales.

Places of interest:
Chester.

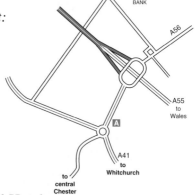

HOOLE BANK

A56

A55
to
Wales

A

A41
to
Whitchurch

to
central
Chester

A Hoole Hall Hotel
Chester.
☎ 01244 350 011

The orginal building was burnt by Cromwell in 1646 but in more recent times in 1785, it was the home of the pioneer balloonist The Rev. Thomas Baldwin. Much later, in the last war it was occupied by the Army and remained derelict for many years.
In 1990 it was rebuilt as a hotel, with 40 single rooms and 57 double bedrooms, and a conference centre. For passing motorists bar meals are available in the lounge bar and an excellent breakfast in the conservatory.

Last orders.
2.30 and 9.15pm.

Price £££

Wolverhampton to Telford

Junctions **1** to **7**

A 23 mile stretch of Motorway which was
opened in 1975 to link Birmingham to
Shrewsbury and Wales. Beyond Telford it has
been upgraded to a modern dual carriageway to
the other side of Shrewsbury.

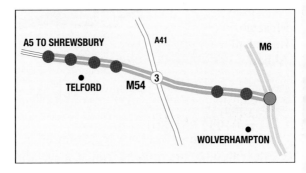

M54 Wolverhampton to Telford

3 Whitchurch Weston A41 Wolverhampton

A rural part of Shropshire. The Bell Inn is almost too easy to find as one can drive past it. Look out for the Murco Filling Station.

Places of interest:
Weston Park. (HHA)
Boscobel House and the Royal
Oak Tree.
Aerospace
Museum.
Lillieshall
Abbey.

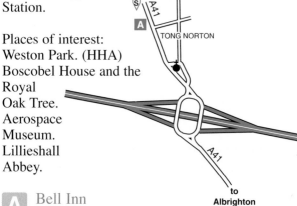

A Bell Inn
Tong,
☎ 01952 851 210

An old Coaching Inn from the 18th century, with some interesting stables. It is now owned by Bank's Brewery and has a restaurant, non smoking bars and a conservatory. Behind there is a beer garden and a playground. Children and dogs are welcome. There are facilities for the disabled.

Last orders. 9pm on Sundays to Wednesdays. 10pm Thursdays to Saturdays.

Price £

Manchester to Chester

M56

Junctions **1** to **16**

Some 37 miles long, it connects Manchester with the commuter areas in Cheshire as well as Chester and North Wales beyond.

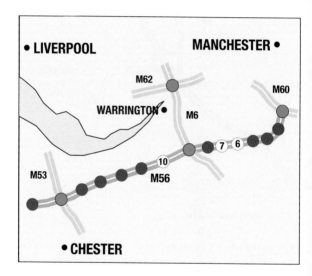

M56

Manchester

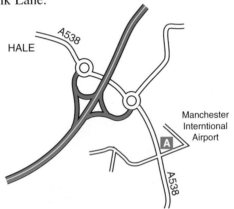

6 Wilmslow Macclesfield Hale
A538

A certain amount of skill is required to negotiate the roundabouts and you may miss the turn off down Sunbank Lane.

HALE

A538

Manchester
Interntional
Airport

A

A538

 The Romper.
Hale Barns.
☎ 01619 806 806.

Owned now by Scottish and Newcastle it was once an old fashioned pub in a backwater, but has been enlarged and modernised. There is a beer garden but the car park is large. Dogs are welcome outside as well as children.

Last orders.
11am to 11pm.
(10.30pm
on Sundays).

Price ££

to Chester

M56

7 Bowdon (A56)

A motorway spur ending at a roundabout. If you are driving westwards, you go over the Motorway and rejoin again at Junction 8. It might be advisable to treat this as a comfort stop.

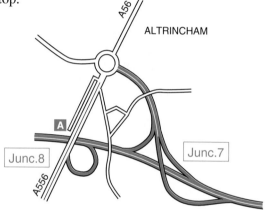

A Nags Head,
Little Bollington.
☎ 01565 830 486.

Once a wayside pub, it is now owned by Noble House and has been modernised to provide a restaurant and a beer garden. A comfort stop.

Last orders.
11am to 10pm
every day.

Price ££

10 Northwich Warrington A559

The Birch and Bottle seems to be further than one expects, but keep on. There are some new purpose built Road Houses visible from the Junction as well.

Places of interest: Anderton Boat Lift. (EH) Arley Hall. (HHA)

LOWER STRETTON

A49

to
Whitchurch

A559

A Ring O' Bells Inn.
Lower Stretton.
☎ 01925 730 556.

Now owned by Namura, it has a friendly atmosphere, but serves no food. Why then is it in the Guide? It is still a typical locals' pub where one gathers for a drink and a gossip.

Last call.
11pm.

Price ££

10 Continued

B Birch and Bottle.
Lower Stretton.
☎ 01925 730 225.

Owned by Greenalls, it is a cheerful place with a restaurant in the conservatory, where you can enjoy their speciality- Black Pudding. This could date from the time when it was built in 1814 as a wayside pub. There is a beer garden for the hardy and his dog.

Last orders.
3 and 11pm.
(10.30 on Sundays).

Price ££

M58
Liverpool

Junctions **1** to **5**

Not the most exciting Motorway, but it fulfills a useful function of linking Liverpool with the M6 going North.

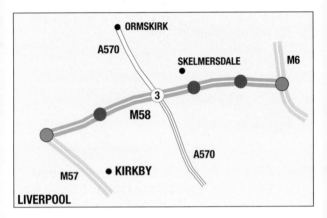

to Wigan

3 St. Helens Ormskirk A570 ⟩

You might miss the Quattro Restaurant, which is on what looks like a layby to the left, as soon as you get off the roundabout.

A Quattro.
Bickerstaffe.
☎ 01695 720 800.

As the name implies, it is an Italian restaurant with the usual cheerful atmosphere. It relies on its food rather than beer gardens and the like, to attract customers of which some fifty can lunch at the same time.
Children and dogs are welcome.

Last orders. 2 and 10.30pm every day, except for Mondays and Saturdays when it is closed for lunch.

Price £££

3 Continued

B The Sandpiper.
Bickerstaffe.
☎ 01695 733 666.

Once a farmhouse, it is now one of the modern
generation of purpose designed pubs, with outside
seating in a garden and a large carpark.
It has a friendly atmosphere and welcomes dogs
outdoors. Bar meals served all day in an open
space bar area, where one can still smoke.

Last food orders. 10pm.
(9.30pm on Sundays).

Price ££

Manchester Orbital

Parts of the ringroad had been known as the M63 and the M62, as well as the M66. It has now been renumbered after the completion of the entire Orbital Motorway as the M60 and the old junction numbers have also been changed. Even the section of the M62, which bypasses Manchester to the north, is numbered M60. It would be best to hurry round Manchester as the only place which gives hint of a comfort stop would be Jacksons Boat at Sale.

M60

Manchester Orbital

6 (ex 8) Sale A144

The access to Jacksons Boat is down a narrow country lane past a Golf Course to the right.

A Jacksons Boat.
Sale.
☎ 0161 973 8549

This must once have been frequented by bargees plying their trade on the River Mersey. At present it has been impossible for the management to find a chef, so for the time being no food is being served. There is a playground and a large beer garden where both dogs and children are allowed.

Price ££

Manchester to Preston

Junctions **1** to **9**

Useful for those living in and around Manchester, going to or coming from the Lake District or the North. Also useful for motorists driving over the Pennines on the M62 to connect with the M1.

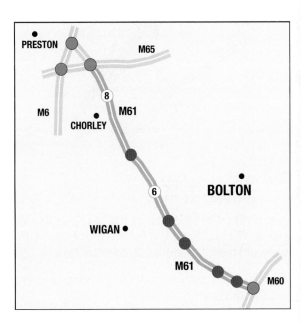

6 Chorley Horwich A6027
Bolton

An uninteresting junction, but the view across to the
Pennines over the Reebok Football Stadium is good.

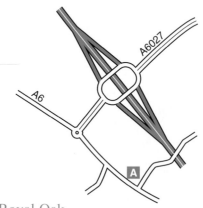

A Royal Oak
West Houghton.
☎ 01942 812 168.

A wayside stop since the 1830s, it is part of a Group
and serves home cooked bar meals all day. A fine
view of Reebok Stadium. A comfort stop.

Last food
orders. 10pm.

Price ££

8 **Blackburn Leyland**
Southport A6

The Red Cat requires
concentration as you
have to drive past it and
then come round behind
it.

to
M65

A

to
Botany Bay

A Red Cat.
Witterly Woods.
☎ 01257 263 966.

There has been a hostelry here since 1805 and is
now a cheerful Italian place obviously
specialising in Italian food served in the
flagstoned eating areas. There is a playground
and a beer garden where dogs are encouraged. It
has recently
changed hands.

Last orders.
2 and 10pm.
11pm on
Sundays.

Price ££

M62

Liverpool to Hull (Trans Pennine Motorway)

Junctions **1** to **38**

One of the few Motorways which runs laterally across the country. It is 108 miles long and links the ports of Liverpool and Hull.

WESTERN SECTION   Junctions 1 - 26

With the best will in the world this part from Liverpool to beyond Manchester is not pretty. However once past junction 21 it climbs up into the Pennines and junction 22 is a remote spot for picnics near the top. Then it descends into the industrial area by Huddersfield.

Liverpool to Hull

9 Newton Warrington A49

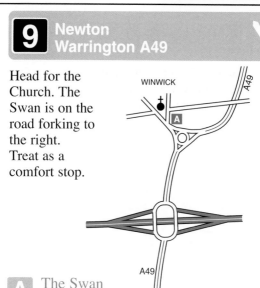

Head for the Church. The Swan is on the road forking to the right.
Treat as a comfort stop.

A The Swan
Winwick.
☎ 01925 631 416.

Apparently there has been a hostelry on the site since the 14th century The present building dates from 1898 and is an offshoot of the Chef and Brewer. There are 42 double bedrooms in a modern extension, with a restaurant and a bar in the older part, serving an imaginative menu. It also caters for conferences. Some outside seating where dogs are permitted.

Last orders. From 12am to 10pm (9.30pm on Sundays).

Price ££

M62

Liverpool

21 Milnrow
Shaw A640

Not as difficult as it looks, but the road through this
ex mining town needs concentration.

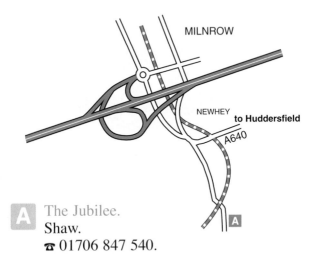

MILNROW

NEWHEY **to Huddersfield**

A640

A The Jubilee.
Shaw.
☎ 01706 847 540.

So named after the Jubilee Colliery which is down
the road but now closed. It is open for lunches only
and closed on Saturday. Privately owned it gives a
friendly welcome to visitors. It specialises in Leg of
Lamb served in the restaurant cum bar. Outside
seating where dogs are welcome.

Last orders. 2.00pm
No meals on
Saturdays.

Price ££

25 Brighouse Dewsbury
Huddersfield A62

Look out for the sign saying Old Corn Mill,
on the right.

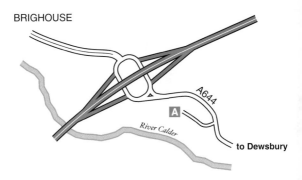

BRIGHOUSE

A644

River Calder

A

to Dewsbury

A The Old Corn Mill
Brighouse.
☎ 01484 400 069.

Once a corn mill as the name implies it is now
family owned and specialises in conferences and
banqueting, as well as having a night club, a
children's playground, a large car park and a
beer garden, as well as outside seating where
dogs are permitted. There is a large area where
bar meals are served. A comfort stop.

Last orders.
2 and 10pm
in the carvery.

Price ££

M62

Liverpool

EASTERN SECTION   **Junctions 27 - 38**

Not the most attractive part of England as it passes through some industrial areas. Even the stretch along the River Humber is rather dull.

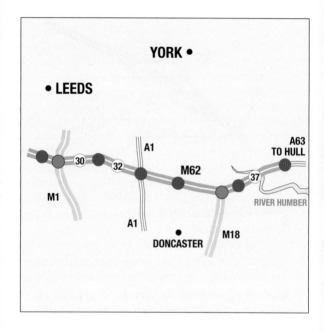

YORK •

• LEEDS

A1

A63
TO HULL

30

32

M62

37

M1

RIVER HUMBER

A1

•
DONCASTER

M18

30 Rothwell
Wakefield A642

Easy enough to find the
Spindle Tree.

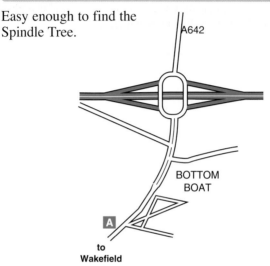

A642

BOTTOM
BOAT

A

to
Wakefield

A Spindle Tree.
Stanley.
☎ 01924 824 810

A small wayside pub owned by Pub Masters. It
has recently been refurbished. Meals are served
in open areas with a bar. Cheerful atmosphere.
Outside seating in a garden at the rear.

Last orders for meals
2.00 and 9.00pm
No evening meals
on Sunday.

Price ££

32 Pontefract Castleford
A639

Handy for those going to the Races, but otherwise a comfort stop.

Places of interest: Pontefract Racecourse.

to Castleford

A639

Pontefract Park Race Course

A

A Parkside Hotel
Pontefract.
☎ 01977 709 911.

A Privately owned hotel opposite the Racecourse, which has 29 bedrooms, a restaurant and a Long Bar where bar meals are served, boasting huge portions of Yorkshire Pudding. A playground, beer garden, outside seating and a large carpark, all of which are overlooked by what was one of the last remaining working coal mine. Once a farm house, it still retains some of its rural heritage.

Last orders.
2.30 and 9.30pm.
(9pm on Sundays).

Price ££

37 Howden A614 Selby A63

Howden was once famous for one of Europe's largest horse fairs. Until some twenty years ago it had degenerated into a one-horse town. It is now a thriving picturesque place.

HOWDEN

Places of interest: Howden Minster. The former summer palace of the Bishops of Durham.

River Ouse

 Wellington Hotel
Howden
☎ 01430 430 258.

Once a Coaching Inn it still gives board and lodging to the passing motorist. It has 3 Single and 7 Double bedrooms, a restaurant and bars where the food is home cooked. Morning coffee and afternoon teas are also available. At the rear is a beer garden where dogs may saunter.

Last orders.
2 and 9.30pm
every day.

Price ££

M65

Preston

Junctions **1** to **14**

For many years the M65 was a short isolated stretch from Colne to Blackburn. It has now been continued to link with the M6 at Preston.

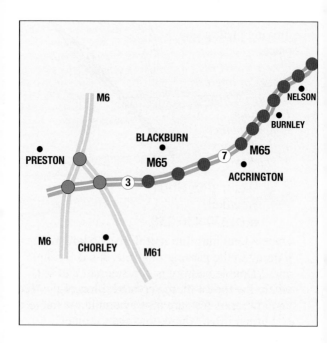

to Colne

M65

3 Blackburn Chorley A674
Bolton A675

The roundabout at the end of the lead off could be confusing.

Places of interest: Hoghton Tower. (HHA)

A Hoghton Arms.
Withnell.
☎ 01254 201 083.

The building has been there since 1704, and has been a pub long before 1910. It has recently been greatly extended to provide more eating areas. A cheerful place with fires, but of the gas fire variety. A restaurant and bar and outside a playground and seating, but dogs are not encouraged.

Last orders.
9pm (8.30pm
on Sundays).

Price ££

207

3 **Continued**

 B The Boatyard Inn
Riley Green
☎ 01254 209 841.

Once a Boat Yard, it has now been converted by
Thwaites Brewery into a waterside inn with large
open areas by the Leeds and Liverpool Canal, where
moorings are available to the intrepid sailor. Dogs
allowed outdoors but children not
encouraged,
for obvious
reasons.

Last orders.
9.30pm every day.
9pm on Fridays.

Price ££

C Ristorante Alghergo
Withnell
☎ 01254 202 222

As the name implies this is an Italian restaurant
which has a good local reputation and a friendly
atmosphere.

Last orders.
10.30pm
(Evenings only)
On Sundays
from 12.00
to 10.00pm.

Price £££

to Colne

7 Clayton le Moors
Accrington A680

Do not be put off by appearing to drive into a factory. Turn left and the Hotel entrance comes into view.

CLAYTON LE MOORS

A378

A

ACCRINGTON

A Macdonald Dunkenhalgh Hotel
Clayton le Moors.
☎ 01254 398 021.

A building has stood here since 1285, but it has been a hotel for some time. It has everything which any self-respecting luxury hotel would have, such as a Leisure Club with a swimming pool, sauna and creature comforts, to relax tired businessmen resting from their conferences there. It has 4 single and 117 double rooms and there are facilities for the disabled. Dogs are permitted within reason. A restaurant, but also a bar serving bar snacks.

Last orders.
9.45pm.
(9pm on
Sundays).

Price ££££

M69

Junctions **1** to **2**

This motorway was built in the mid 1970s to give direct access between Coventry and Leicester. It is comparatively little used so is useful to those who are using the M1 and M40 as a means of driving north or south.

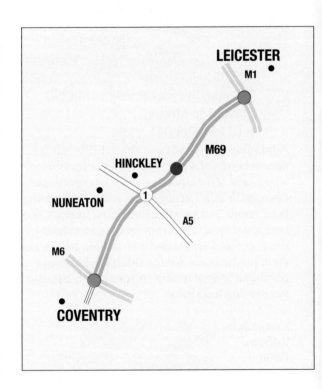

to Leicester

 Nuneaton Lutterworth A5

This Exit intersects with the A5 -the Roman
Watling Street – which until the building of
the M1 and the M6 was the main road to
Birmingham.

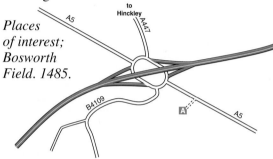

*Places
of interest;
Bosworth
Field. 1485.*

A Barnacles Restaurant
Nr Hinckley
☎ 01455 633 220.

A privately owned Restaurant in pleasant
grounds with a lake. It specialises in fish food
and there is a separately owned shop next to
the restaurant which sells fish. Dogs are not
welcomed and there are no special facilities
for children.

Last orders.
1.45 and
9.30pm.

Price £££

M180

Doncaster

Junctions **1** to **5**

A short 27 mile stretch from the M18 to Grimsby, the last 15 miles being dual carriageway. Junction 5, the present end of the Motorway, is also the turnoff for the Humber Bridge on the A15 dual carriageway. Neither the Bridge nor the Motorway are overcrowded.

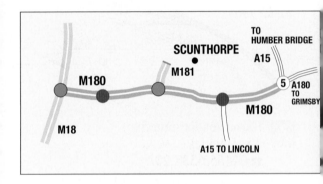

to Grimsby (Humber Bridge) M180

5 Humber Bridge
Humber Airport A18

This is the end of the
Motorway, but it is a
good road to the
Humber Bridge
and to Grimsby.

*Places of interest:
Elsham Hall and
Country Park.*

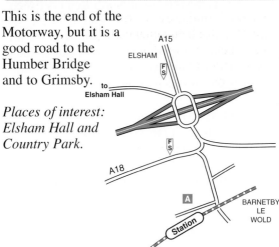

A The Whistle & Flute.
Barnetby Le Wold.
☎ 01652 688 238.

Opposite the station which still functions, but
not too noisily. It is a family owned hotel which
has 10 double bedrooms. There is a restaurant
and a bar where home cooked food and fresh
vegetables are served. Outside there is a
playground and seating where children
and dogs may roam.

Last orders.
2 and 9.30pm.
2.30 and 9pm
on Sundays.

Price ££

A1(M)

London

Junctions 6 to 63

The A1 was the old Great North Road between London and Edinburgh. The building of the M1 and the M6 reduced its importance, but with the level of traffic rising, efforts were and are being made to upgrade it to Motorway standard. At the moment only six sections have been so modernised but the numbering of the Exits is on the basis that they will all be linked up eventually. These sections are the southern part from the M25 to Baldock; the Peterborough section, the Doncaster section; the junction with the M1; the Boroughbridge part and lastly from Scotch Corner to Newcastle.

SOUTHERN SECTION   Junctions 1 - 10

A boring stretch getting out of London.

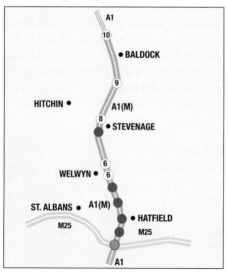

6 Welwyn Garden City A1000

A complicated system of roundabouts, but worth the effort as Welwyn (as opposed to Welwyn Garden City) is a pleasant market town to this day.

Places of interest:
The Roman Baths and
George Bernard Shaw's
house at Ayton
St Lawrence.

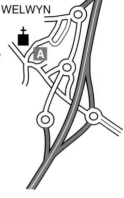

WELWYN

A The White Hart.
Welwyn.
☎ 01438 715 353.

Once a Georgian Coaching Inn, it no longer has bedrooms, but concentrates on bar meals for local businessmen. It has a restaurant and bar and specialises in Roast Beef and fresh vegetables. Lunches only.

Last orders.
2pm.
Closed on
Sundays.

Price ££

Stevenage was once a sleepy country town and then became one of the first New Towns. There is little reason to go through it, unless to visit Knebworth House, for which Exit 7 is closest. The village of Little Wymondley is attractive in rather a chintzy way but nevertheless pleasant. Graveley on the Old Great North Road has changed little.

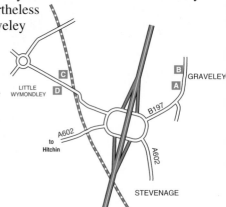

A George and Dragon
Graveley
☎ 01438 351 362

An old Georgian house which might have been a Coaching Inn, but is now an unassuming village pub but with golfing memorabilia. It has a restaurant and bar and some outside seating. Children and dogs (the latter on leads) are welcome.
A comfort stop.

Last orders 2.30
and 9.30pm
including
Sundays.

Price £££

8 Continued

B The Wagon and Horses
Graveley
☎ 01438 367 658

Next door to the George and Dragon, it was most probably a coaching stop. It has a beer garden where there are barbecues on those rare summer evenings. Children and dogs are welcome. A comfort stop.

Last orders
2.30 and 8.30pm,
but 9pm on Fridays
and Saturdays.
No lunches on
Sundays.

Price ££

C Plume of Feathers
Little Wymondley
☎ 01438 729 503

A small 18th Century house which makes a comfortable pub. It has a restaurant and a bar; a children's playground and outside seating where you can watch a game of Petanque. Children and dogs are welcome.

Last orders
2 and 9.15pm.
No evening meals
on Sundays

Price ££

8 Continued

D The Bucks Head
Little Wymondley
☎ 01438 353 320

It has been an inn since it was built some 400 years ago. It seems to have everything such as a children's playground, a family room, outside seating, a car park and Petanque. Children and dogs are welcome.

Last orders 2.15 and 9.30pm (9pm on Sundays).

Price £

9 Baldock Letchworth A6141 ╲

For those coming from the south one would turn off here for Baldock, which is an attractive town with predominantly Georgian architecture. Conversely, those driving down from the north would come off at Exit 10.

to Baldock

A

A6141

A George IV
Baldock
☎ 01462 892 367.

The Manager of this wayside pub, on the outskirts of the town, was a fishmonger, so he specialises in fish. It has a childrens playground, a beer garden where on summer nights when it is warm enough, there is a barbeque. Children, but not dogs are welcome. There is a live Blues Band on Monday nights and Jazz on Saturdays. At other times you can feed the squirrels.

Last orders.
2.30 and 9pm
every day.

Price ££

PETERBOROUGH SECTION Junctions 13 - 17

The most recent part of the A1(M) to be built to motorway standards. It is unusual in having four lanes which could be a sign of future growth in traffic.

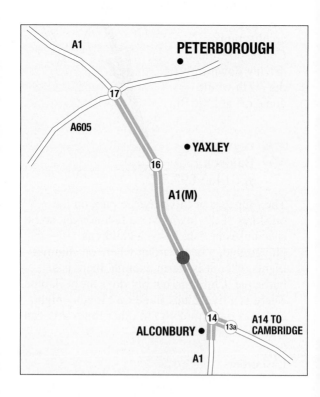

13/14 Alconbury Huntingdon A14

A difficult Exit but it is a way for those driving up from the south to switch over to the A14 to go to Cambridge. For those trying to regain the road going north, you have to go through the same procedure, but head north on the A14 which then rejoins the A1.

Attractions; Ramsey Abbey Gatehouse (NT)
Monks Wood Nature Reserve.

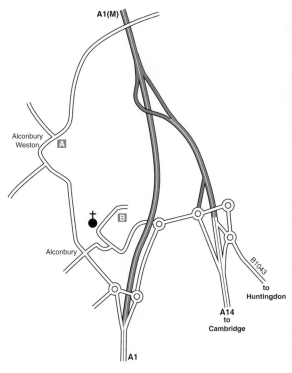

221

13 Continued

A The White Hart
Alconbury Weston
☎ 01480 890 331

A pleasant rural village pub. No particular facilities except a dart board but a friendly atmosphere. No children but dogs outdoors. Bar meals only.

Last orders 2 and 9pm.
(9.30pm on Fridays and
Saturdays.
No evening meals
on Sundays.

Price ££

B The Manor House Hotel
Alconbury
☎ 01480 890 423

A 17th Century house now a privately owned pub/hotel. It has a restaurant and bar with a garden at the rear. There are 4 double bedrooms. No children or dogs.

Last orders
2 and 9pm.
No evening meals
on Sundays.

Price ££

16 Peterborough A15

The Exit is easy, but finding one's way through
Yaxley is more difficult.

*Attractions. Peterborough Cathedral Elton Hall
(HHA) Southwick Hall
(HHA)*

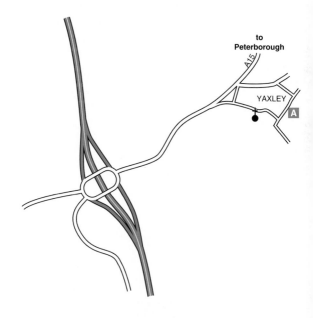

16 Continued

A Three Horseshoes
Yaxley
☎ 01733 242 059

A cosy pub on the main street of the village which is
now in reality a dormitory of Peterborough. It serves
bar meals from a menu and has a children's
playground, beer garden and a car park at the rear.
Shielded from a small caravan park by a leylandia
hedge.

Last orders
2 and 9pm. 9.30pm
on Fridays and Saturdays.

Price £

to Newcastle **A1(M)**

DONCASTER SECTION Junctions 34-38

One of the original sections to be rebuilt as a
motorway. It is also a junction to the M18 which
links the M1 to the M62 and Hull.

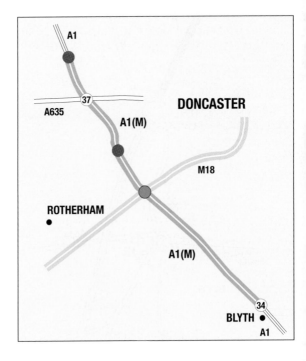

A1(M) London

34 Bawtry A614 Worksop B6045

An easy Exit, but for those driving up from the south, it is best to get off onto the slip road a mile or so beforehand.

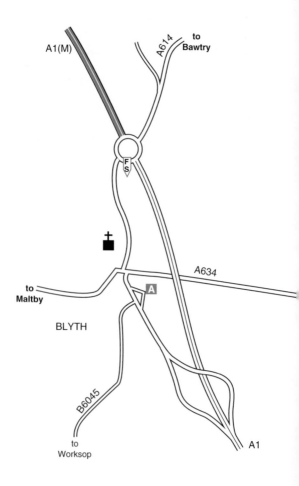

226

 Continued

 White Swan
Blyth
☎ 01909 591 222.

A small pub overlooking the village green, with
some outside seating. It serves bar meals
especially fish and the rest is home made. Dogs
are discouraged, due to the resident hounds, as
well as children as it is too small to cope.

Last orders 2
and 9.30pm
every day except
Sunday evenings.

Price ££

A1(M)   London

37 Barnsley
Doncaster A635

A straightforward Exit posing no problems. A filling station just beyond Marr Lodge.

Places of interest: Brodsworth Hall (EH)
Cusworth Hall

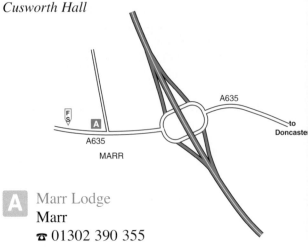

A Marr Lodge
Marr
☎ 01302 390 355

A modern building, but it caters for the passing motorist, especially those on their way to or from Brodsworth Hall. It serves bar type meals in various open plan bars. Most of the food is home made. No dogs, but children welcome.

Last orders.
All day until
11pm, except
Sundays which
is 10.30pm.

Price ££

WETHERBY SECTION Junctions 44 - 49

This section is in two parts, both of recent construction. The southern section is the junction with the recently completed M1 extension. The A1 between 45 and 46 is dual carriageway throughout.

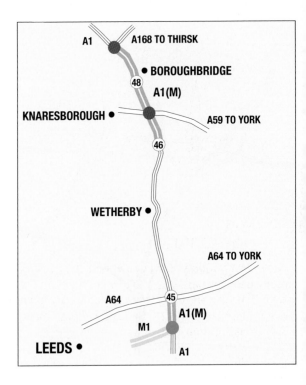

London

45 Leeds
Tadcaster A64

Junction 44 to the south is where the M1 bears off
from the A1. Exit 45 is a normal sort of layout.
Those going to Bramham on the dual carriageway
come off the A1 as they would with a motorway.

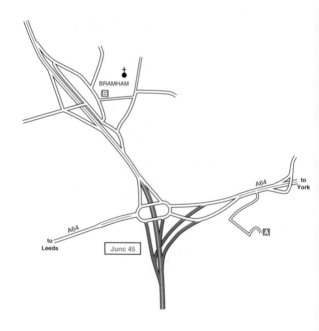

to Newcastle A1(M)

45 Continued

A Hazelwood Castle Hotel
Hazelwood
☎ 01937 535 353

An imposing pile in 77 acres of grounds dating
from the Domesday Book which was crenellated
in 1290. It has recently been converted into an
elegant hotel with 21 bedrooms. It was
previously occupied by Carmelite Monks, who
would have had a simpler life style than that
now offered, which includes the 1086
Restaurant, a Cookery School, conference and
banquet suites, musical events and Clay Pigeon
shoots. For those in more of a rush there is the
Prickly Pear Bistro. Morning coffee, breakfasts
and afternoon teas are available .

Last orders 9.45pm in the Restaurant (which
does not serve lunch, except on Sundays). The
Bistro is open all day from 11am to 9.30pm.

Price ££££

45 Continued

B The Red Lion
Bramham
☎ 01937 843 524

A typical village pub, which has been extended by annexing the butchers shop next door as a restaurant. A cheerful place with attentive service. A beer garden and car park. Children and dogs welcome.

Last orders 2 and 8.45pm. No evening meals on Sunday.

Price ££

47 Knaresborough Harrogate York A59

This Exit is really only for those travelling north, as it is easy to get off for the Bridge Inn Hotel, 9 miles to the South.

Places of interest: Marston Moor 1644. Knaresborough Castle (EH) Mother Shipton's Cave. Allerton Castle (HHA) Stockeld Park (HHA).

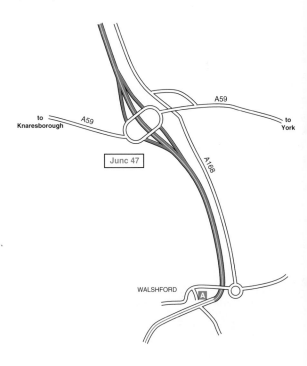

47 Continued

A The Bridge Inn and Hotel
Walshford
☎ 01937 580 115

A privately owned hotel with a Restaurant/ Carvery and several bars. There are 29 double bedrooms (two of which are reserved for disabled) and a gym. Another claim to fame is that the Dining Room of Holraby Hall (demolished 1951), which was the scene of Lord Byrons disastrous first night of his honeymoon, was re-erected here. The original inn is still there and serves bar meals.

Last orders 2.30 and 9.45pm (9pm on Sundays)
No lunch in the restaurant on Saturdays.

Price £££

to Newcastle A1(M)

48 Knaresborough A6055
Boroughbridge A168

A dumbbell form of Exit with roundabouts at each end. Boroughbridge was a coaching stop on the Great North Road.

Places of interest: Roman town of Isurium.

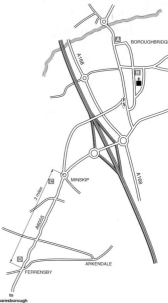

A The Crown
Boroughbridge
☎ 01423 322 328

An old coaching inn since 1672, once with stabling for a hundred horses. It has now been modernised to have accommodation with 35 double and 2 single bedrooms. It also has a swimming pool, sauna and gym to relax tired motorists. A comfortable restaurant and bars. No dogs.

Last orders 9.30pm. No lunches in the restaurant except on Saturdays.

Price ££

235

48 Continued

 B The Dining Room
Boroughbridge
☎ 01423 326 426

A family owned restaurant in the centre of the town, which was opened some two years ago. It is small and comfortable with an imaginative menu. Well behaved children and dogs allowed. Advisable to reserve.

Last orders
2.00 and 9.00pm
No evening meals
on Sundays.

Price £££

 C White Swan
Minskip
☎ 01423 322 598

A small village pub with a friendly atmosphere. It specialises in home cooking and Yorkshire Puddings. There is a children's playground and beer garden at the rear. Dogs are welcome.

Last orders
2 and 9.30pm.

Price ££

48 Continued

D General Tarleton
Ferrensby
☎ 01423 340 284

A privately owned restaurant and hotel with 14
bedrooms. It is reputed to have the best cuisine
in Yorkshire with a warm welcome from a
young professional staff in a relaxed
atmosphere. Dogs and children welcome
provided they behave.

Last food orders
2.15 and 9.30pm
8.30 on Sundays.

Price £££*

A1(M)

London

---

49 **Thirsk A168 Ripon**

You can get off the A168 and return to the A1 easily enough, provided you follow the plan.

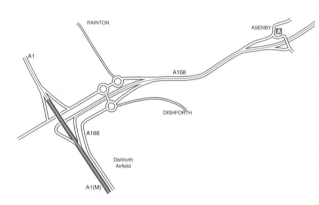

A The Crab and Lobster
Asenby
☎ 01845 577 286

One of the best places for a stopover on a motorway! The decor has been done with flair and the set menu (which obviously specialises in fish) is excellent value for money. There is outside seating under umbrellas, hopefully against the sun. An added plus is that Crab Manor, in the same ownership next door, is an 11 bedroom hotel with a delightful mix of furniture and styles.

Last food orders
2.15 and 9.15 pm
2.00 and 9.00 pm
on Sundays.

Price ££££*

to Newcastle

NEWCASTLE SECTION   Junc 56 - 63

The most northerly section, starting at Scotch
Corner and ending south of Gateshead. Not
particularly attractive – but one passes close to
the Angel of the North.

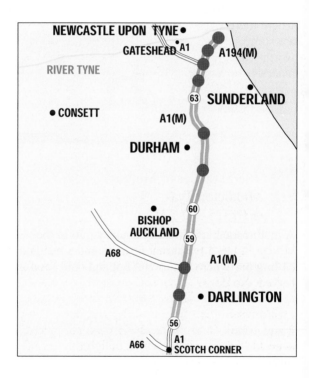

56 Scotch Corner A1
Bishop Auckland B6275

There are no pubs near this Exit, but two miles to the south is the junction with the A66 known as Scotch Corner, where there are some worthwhile places.

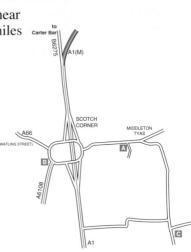

A The Shoulder of Mutton

Middleton Tyas

☎ 01325 377 271

A picturesque and friendly country pub in the village, it has a restaurant upstairs and a beamed ceiling bar where traditional hot and cold food is served. No dogs.

Last orders 2 and 10pm every day including Sundays.

Price £££

56 Continued

B Scotch Corner Hotel
Scotch Corner
☎ 01748 850 900

Scotch Corner was a historical landmark, where
you made the decision whether to brave it over
the Pennines on the way to Carlisle, or play it
safe especially in the winter and go to
Edinburgh via Newcastle. Today it is owned by
a hotel chain and has been modernised. As a
result it has a restaurant, bars and a carvery. For
the overnighters there are 72 double and 18
single bedrooms, a swimming pool, sauna and
jacuzzi. Children, dogs, coaches and the
disabled are all catered for.

Last orders 2 and 9.30pm every day.

Price ££££

56 Continued

C The Black Bull
Moulton
☎ 01325 377 289

One of the best known places in this part of
Yorkshire and privately owned. It has a conservatory
restaurant as well as several dining areas and a bar
which serves bar meals. In addition to these there is
Hazel - a pullman carriage from the Brighton Belle,
which is used for dinners. No children under 7. It is
advisable to book.

Last orders 2 and 10pm every day but closed
Sundays.

Price ££££*

59 Darlington
Newton Aycliffe A167

To get to The County turn right at the traffic
lights and right again onto the village green.

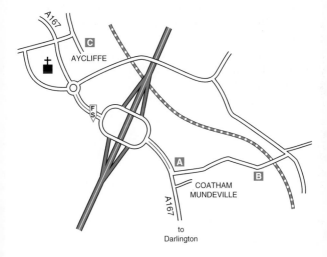

Foresters Arms
Coatham Mundeville
☎ 01325 320 565

A typical country pub, but with a small restaurant
and bars. Outside there is a children's playground and
seating, when the sun shines. Dogs are however
not welcomed.

Last orders are
3 and 9.45pm.
Closed Sunday
evenings.

Price £

 Hall Garth Country Hotel
Coatham Mundeville
☎ 01325 300 400

An imposing old mansion dating back to 1684. It is
now surrounded by a golf course but its original
gardens are still there. It has 40 double bedrooms but
a new wing with a further 10 bedrooms and a
function room has recently been added. Residents
can use the swimming pool and the Leisure Centre.
The Old Stables Bar serves bar snacks. Dogs are
welcome.

Last orders
2 and 9.30pm
(9pm on Sundays).

Price ££££

59 Continued

C The County
Aycliffe Village
☎ 01325 312 273

A country style pub on the village green which was probably a coaching stop when the A.1 passed through Aycliffe. Within the past three years the owner, Andrew Brown, has transformed it into a civilized place for meals and a convivial evening. It recently came into public notice as Tony Blair brought President Chirac of France to have dinner here. Restricted outside seating. Children suffered but not dogs. French not essential.

Last orders 2 and 9.30pm
No evening meals on Sundays.

Price £££

A1(M)

London

60 — Bishop Auckland Hartlepool Teeside A689

An easy Exit and the Hotel is signed from the Exit.

Places of interest:
Bishop Auckland
Palace (HHA)
Sedgefield
Racecourse.

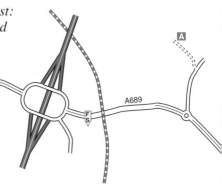

A Hardwick Hall Hotel
Sedgefield
☎ 01740 620 253

Once an 18th Century mansion, it still stands in its original grounds of 120 acres, which are now listed Grade II*. During the last war it was a Convalescent Home for soldiers and then became a Maternity Hospital. It has been enlarged and extended into a hotel where visitors continue to be well cared for in one of the 50 bedrooms. There is a restaurant, conference facilities and a bar called the Inn on the Park. A golf course is next door. Children but no dogs.

Last orders
2 and 9.30pm
either in the
restaurant
or in the Bistro.

Price ££££

to Newcastle **A1(M)**

63 Chester Le Street

An easy Exit to start with as Lumley Castle is signed. Then the signs disappear, but keep bearing left and they will reappear.

Places of interest: St Peters Church in Chester le Street (where St Cuthberts body rested for a 100 years before final burial at Durham Cathedral). Beamish Open Air Museum.

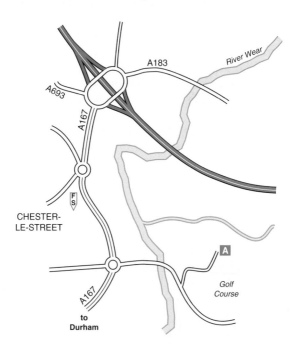

63 Continued

A Lumley Castle
Chester Le Street
☎ 1091 389 1111

Built in 1389 by Sir Ralph Lumley, it is still owned by the family, although now leased for the past 25 years and turned into a friendly, efficient and comfortable hotel. Today it has 59 bedrooms and the Great Hall is still used for its original purpose to welcome guests for a meal but there are other excellent restaurants. It is surrounded by 9 acres of garden and over the road there is a golf course. Although the bedrooms are all plumbed, it has been impossible to install lifts through the roof structures and massive walls. Children but no dogs.

Last orders 2 and 9.30pm every day, but no lunches on Saturday.

Price ££££*

Horndean to Portsmouth A3(M)

Junctions **1** to **5**

A short stretch of motorway, completed in 1979, to ease the junction of the A3 to the M27.

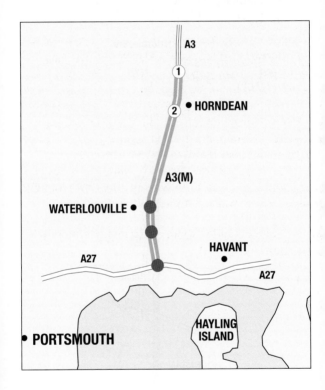

2 Horndean
Cowplain B2149

Coming from the north take the slip road to
Horndean and get on again at the Exit 2 further
south. It could be a little complicated.

*Places
of interest:
Stansted
Park (HHA)*

to Guildford
& London

A3

*Southbound
access only*

B

Brewery

A

A3(M)

HORNDEAN

B2149

Junc 2

to
Rowland's
Castle

C

250

to Portsmouth A3(M)

2 Continued

A The Ship and Bell Hotel.
Horndean
☎ 02392 592 107.

It is owned by George Gale Brewery literally next door, so one can be assured of the quality of the beer and you can tour the Brewery on request. It has been a Coaching Inn since 1671, and was probably the last stop for Nelson's officers before joining their ships. It has 14 bedrooms, a restaurant, two bars and serves home cooked fare. Dogs are welcome in this traditional old English hotel, which has seen kinder days. A comfort stop.

Last orders. 2.30 and 9.30pm.
No evening meals
on Sundays.

Price ££

B The Anchor Inn
Horndean
☎ 02392 591 050

A family owned locals pub, with a bar and restaurant, serving Real Ale and Steak and Guinness Pie. Outside seating and children's play area. A comfort stop.

Last food
orders.
2.45 and
9.00pm.

Price £

251

2 **Continued**

C The Robin Hood
Rowlands Castle
☎ 02392 412 268.

It has recently opened as a restaurant and is just within five minutes from the junction. A friendly atmosphere, light and airy, looking out over the village green where horses are not allowed to be ridden. Outside seating with heaters if required and where children and dogs are welcome. Private car park at the rear.

Last orders 2.00 and 9.00pm.

Price £££*

SCOTLAND

Motorway Introduction

Scotland may extend a warm welcome to visitors and even Sassenachs, but to the motorway user one gets the impression that the Scots have forgotten the art of hospitality to the passing traveller.

Part of this impression may be due to the fact that the new Motorways, except for the M74 do not follow the old coaching routes, but the same can be said for England. There are some excellent exceptions to the rule, but there were a lot which did not come up to scratch. On the M8 for example, from Edinburgh to Glasgow, there is not one single place worthy of being mentioned. The most tedious aspect of the Scottish motorways was the system of linked Junctions. It might save money, but it generates unnecessary driving on minor roads, especially when one gets lost.

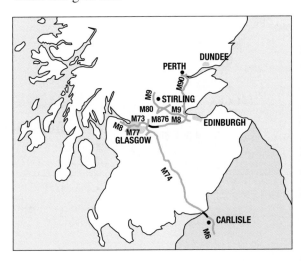

Edinburgh

Junctions **1** to **11**

Starting near the Airport it passes through agricultural country and old shale heaps, before you drive past the impressive ruins of Linlithgow Palace, it ends north of the equally impressive Stirling Castle.

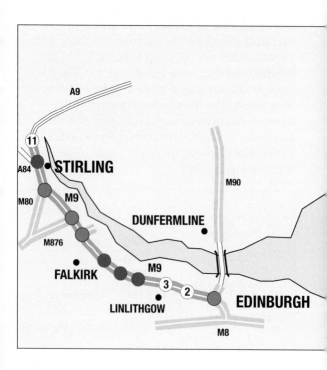

to Stirling

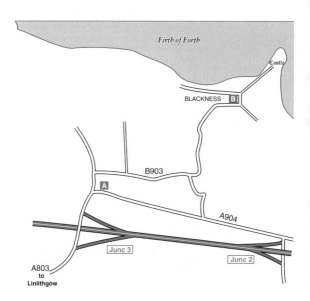

2&3 2. South Queensferry A904
3. Linlithgow Bo'ness A904

Like most of the Junctions these are linked
together, depending upon the direction of travel.
Apart from the two mentioned below, there are
other places in Linlithgow to suit most
requirements.

Places of Interest: Hopetoun House, (HHA)
The House of The Binns. (NTS)
Blackness Castle,(HS) Linlithgow Palace.(HS)

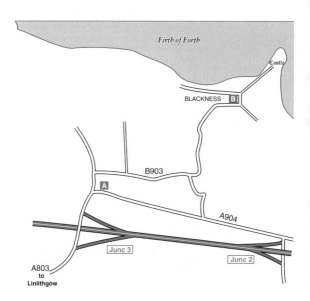

 Continued

A Champany Inn.
Champany.
☎ 01506 834 532.

One of the best known restaurants in Scotland, it was once a farm house where Mary Queen of Scots used to come over from Linlithgow to have picnics, hence the name. The Inn also has 16 bedrooms should one not be tempted to drive on again after dinner. There is outside seating for hot days and a Bistro to suit the more hurried motorist. It is noted for Aberdeen Angus beef and has been named as Meat Restaurant of Great Britain as well as Best Restaurant of the Year.

Last orders. 2 and 10pm.
The main restaurant is not
open on Sundays
nor Saturday Lunch.

Price ££££*

2&3 Continued

B The Blackness Inn
Blackness.
☎ 01506 834 252.

A privately owned pub specialising in sea food.
It was built in the 1700s, and at one stage was
burnt down. The welcome which is homely with
wooden floor, tables and chairs includes dogs
and children. It has recently changed hands.

Last orders. 2 and 8.30pm,
but closed on Mondays.
and Saturday Lunch.

Price £££

11 **Doune B824 Dunblane B8033 Bridge of Allan A9**

The turn off for the Inn is just before one crosses over the bridge.

Places of Interest: Doune Castle. Stirling Castle.(HS) Argyll's Lodging (HS) Safari Park.
The Wallace Monument.

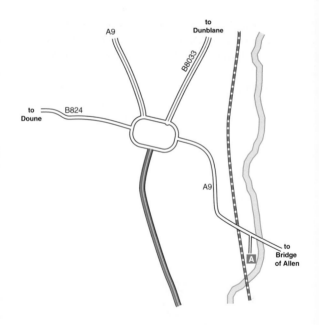

Continued

A The Old Bridge Inn.
Bridge of Allan.
☎ 01786 833 335.

The Inn was built in 1710 by the bridge which was first constructed in 1520 and rebuilt in 1695. It was originally surrounded by mills and by Willie's brewery, famous for making good beer. The interior has been stripped out to make a larger area with rough stone walls and timber panelling. There is an uncommonly fine foliated stone mantlepiece which must have arrived from elsewhere. The owner collects old typewriters and home cine projectors. A bell from the Temple Church in Glasgow will let customers know when they have overstayed their welcome.

Last orders.
2.30 and 8.45pm
every day.

Price £££

M74

Glasgow

Junctions **4** to **24**

Work to upgrade the old A74 has been going on for what seems to be decades. Within the last few years however most of it has now been rebuilt. In places it still refers to itself as an A road. This could be due to a reluctance to spend money replacing the old signs. There also seems to be a reluctance to join up with the M6 to make it a continuous Motorway, but perhaps there is a hidden agenda to keep the system independent and uncontaminated by the English roads and numbering.

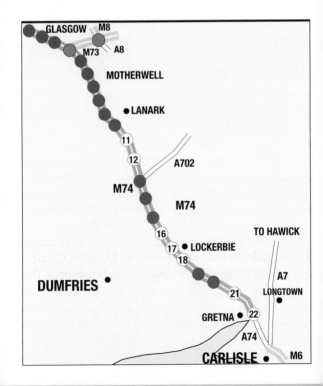

11&12 Douglas Edinburgh A70

Another of the maddening split road junctions, so that Junctions 11 and 12 must be read as one.

Places of Interest: St Brides Church.

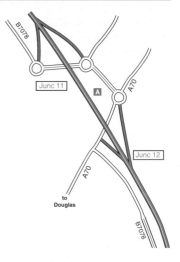

A Cairn Lodge Services.
Happendon.
☎ 01555 851 177.

This is the only Motorway Service area included in the guide. It is privately owned and although it has the usual requirements for the modern traveller, such as a Games section and shops, it nevertheless has tried to be more comfortable and original. It also has the advantage of a good view from the restaurant section, of the Lodge gates to Douglas Castle (Demolished in the 1960s) which had been the formal entrance to the castle grounds.

Last orders. 6.30am through to 10pm every day.

Price ££

17 Lockerbie B7078 Dumfries (A709)

An easy Junction. You can see the Hotel as soon as you get off the Motorway.

Places of Interest:
Lochmaben Castle (HS)
Rammerscales. (HHA)

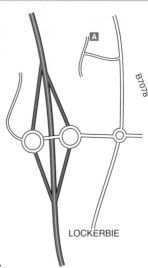

B7078

LOCKERBIE

A Dryfesdale Hotel.
Nr Lockerbie.
☎ 01576 202 427.

The house was built in the late 17th century as the Manse, but was converted into a hotel in the early 1900s. It is privately owned and has recently changed hands. It has 3 single and 12 double bedrooms and some are capable of being used by the disabled. A restaurant and bar cater for lunch and dinners. Morning breakfast for the passing motorist. A helipad is now part of the scene. Dogs are warmly welcomed.

Last orders.
2 and 9pm
every day.

Price ££

to Carlisle

18 Lockerbie B723 Dumfries (A709)

Another restricted
Junction, so for
those driving
north you have
to rejoin at
Junction 17.

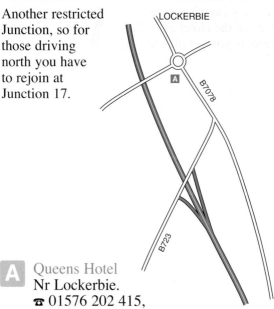

LOCKERBIE

B7078

B723

A Queens Hotel
Nr Lockerbie.
☎ 01576 202 415,

Once a private house it was converted into a
hotel and has now grown to an extent that
modern annexes had to be added and there is
now a leisure centre as well, with a swimming
pool. Outside there is a playground as well as a
beer garden and seating. The disabled, children
and dogs are all more than welcome. A comfort
stop.

Last orders.
2.30 and 9pm,
every day.

Price ££

263

M74 — Glasgow

21 — Annan / Canonbie B6357

Not an easy Junction to follow, but at least you can get on and off it from both directions.

Junc 21

B7078

B6357

Roman Road

KIRKPATRICK FLEMING

to Annan

A

Junc 22

A The Mill
Grahamshill
☎ 01461 800 344.

The Mill started life as a farmhouse in 1740 and was converted into a hotel and restaurant in the 1990s. It has 4 single and 23 double rooms and children and dogs are welcome. It has a restaurant and a bar all on one level so it is disabled friendly. It only serves dinners and there are no lunches.

Last orders. 8.45pm.

Price ££

264

to Carlisle

22 Longton A6071
Gretna Green B7076

Really for those coming from the south and
even then it is a marathon getting back onto the
Motorway. Those driving down from the north
deserve a medal for map-reading to reach the
hotel.

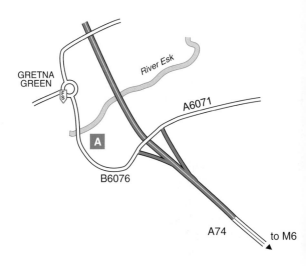

22 Continued

A The Gretna Chase Hotel
Gretna Green.
☎ 01461 337 517.

The first or last hotel in England. It was built in 1865
by the owner of the Toll Bar over the river to house
runaway couples who had to spend a statutory 2
weeks in residence before being allowed to wed
there. One wonders what action they took when irate
parents arrived on the scene. It is still a family run
hotel with 9 double bedrooms and 2 acres of well
kept garden. A comfortable restaurant and bar where
morning coffee and afternoon teas can be had by
those merely in need of refreshment. Dogs allowed
but outdoors.

Last orders. 3 and 9,30pm every day.

Price £££ ⊨

Edinburgh to Perth

Junctions 1 to 10

The most inviting of the Scottish Motorways, as after leaving Edinburgh you cross over the Forth suspension bridge with the imposing old rail bridge to the right. You pass Loch Leven, where Queen Mary was imprisoned, before coming over the high ground by Glenfarg and look down onto Perth and beyond it, the Highlands. A note of caution, at Junction 10 it splits – one part towards Dundee – the other, to the west of Perth.

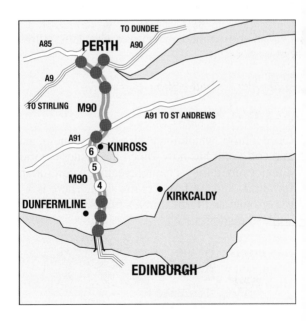

M90

Edinburgh

4 Kelty B914

You can see the
Butterchurn
from the
Motorway,
coming from
the South.

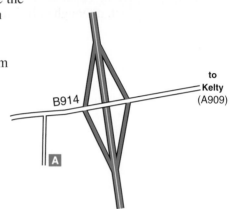

B914

to
Kelty
(A909)

A The Butterchurn.
Kelty.
☎ 01383 830 169.

Once a farm, which then started a sideline in teas
and coffees, it has now joined the modern world with
a major rebuilding scheme, creating a comfortable
restaurant and a gift and crafts shop. There is a
playground and farm animals roam around as
well, so no dogs.

Last orders;
From 9am to 9pm.
High Teas
between 4.30
and 6pm.

Price £££

5 Cleish B9097

An easy exit but the Hotel seems further than you would expect, although only 2 miles.

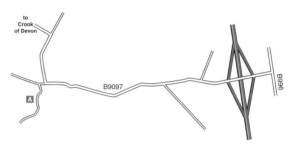

A Nivingston House Hotel,
Cleish
☎ 01577 850 216

A family owned hotel set in 12 acres of garden at the foot of the Cleish Hills. The Victorian facade masks the original building of 1725. It has 3 single and 6 double rooms with a restaurant, bar and a lounge. Morning coffee and afternoon teas for the passing motorist. Children and dogs permitted.

Last orders;
 2 and 9pm.

Price £££*

6 Kinross A977

The private road to the Grouse and Claret is opposite the Esso Filling Station. If it is full, there are at least four good hotels in Kinross.

Places of Interest:
Loch Leven
Castle.(HS)
Kinross House
Garden (HHA)

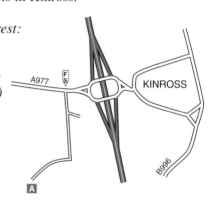

 The Grouse and Claret,
Heatheryford.
☎ 01577 864 212.

A surprisingly peaceful spot, with a large garden looking onto a small loch. An imaginative menu, with a hint of the East, (but specialising in venison, salmon; fish and cheese souffles) in a comfortable restaurant with a bar. For the famished in mind, there is an art gallery.

Last orders:
2.30 and 7pm.
Closed on Sundays
in winter.

Price £££*

Bonnybridge to Kincardine Bridge (M9)

M876

Junctions **1** to **3**

A short stretch of Motorway linking the M80 with Kincardine Bridge and intersecting with the M9.

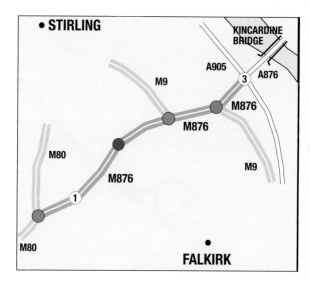

M876 Bonnybridge

 Denny Falkirk A883

Easy enough going north, but you must heed the plan, coming south. The entry onto the motorway going south is not marked at the roundabout.

Places of interest: The Roman Antonine Wall (Rough Castle) (NTS).

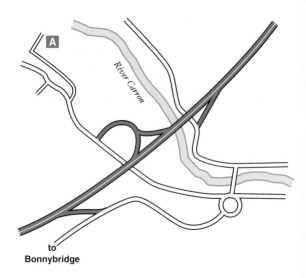

1 Continued

A The Horsemill Inn and Woodyeat Farm.
Denny
☎ 01324 822 241.

Once a farmhouse built in the 1700s, the name implies that horsepower drove the machinery, which in some farmhouses can still be seen. It is family owned and run, with a restaurant and a bar, a playground and outside seating. There is a games room for the children on wet days, but dogs are not allowed. High Teas are served on Saturdays and Sundays from 5 to 7pm.

Last orders. 2.30 and 9pm every day, but closed on Mondays.

Price £££

M876 Bonnybridge

3 Kincardine Stirling A905

The motorway ends at the roundabout, but continues as the A876 to Kincardine Bridge.

Places of interest: The Pineapple, Dunmore Park (NTS).

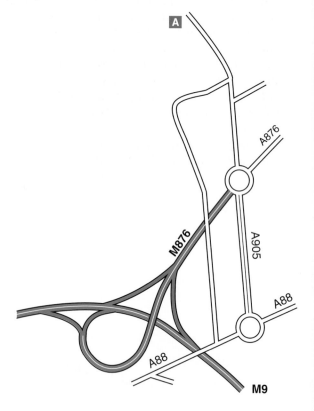

3 **Continued**

 A Airth Castle and Hotel.
Airth.
☎ 01324 831 411

Once the castle home, since the 14th century, of the Barons of Airth and Lords of Elphinstone, it is now a 4 Star hotel owned by Radisson SAS. The original castle has 23 bedrooms and a restaurant, whilst over at the former stables, now fully converted, there is a further 99 bedrooms and another restaurant, together with a Cocktail Bar. As one would expect, it has everything the modern motorist would wish for, including a fully equipped leisure centre, conference centre and banqueting for 240 diners. The gardens surrounding the castle and the view over towards Falkirk are good, but the whole setting is slightly marred by a proliferation of newly built Executive housing in the immediate grounds. The disabled are catered for and children and dogs are welcome.

Last orders. 2 and 10pm.

Price £££

ACKNOWLEDGEMENTS

I would like to thank Cadogan Guides for their permission to reuse some of the original illustrations which appeared in "5 Minutes Off the Motorway." first printed in 1995 and for relinquishing their rights to this publication.

Thanks are due to the Highways Agency, The Historic Houses Association, English Heritage and Historic Scotland, The National Trust and the National Trust for Scotland, for their assistance or for suggesting places of interest near a Junction.

My gratitude is due to the many others without whose help this guide could not have been produced. My thanks especially to my brother Paul for redrawing the plans and to Tracy Coxon, who toiled long and hard to transfer old fashioned typing and drawings to modern methods of printing. Thanks also are due to Jon Bessant and his colleagues of Stephens & George Limited for their technical assistance.

Finally my thanks are due to those readers who have made a valuable contribution to this Edition.

ALPHABETICAL INDEX

INDEX *continued*

INDEX *continued*

NAME	M'WAY	EXIT	PAGE
Foresters Arms	A1(M)	59	244
Fox	M5	17	74
Fox & Hounds	M6	18	94
Fox & Hounds	M40	10	164
Frombridge Mill	M5	13	70
Gables Hotel	M5	14	73
Garden Restaurant	M2	7	25
Gaydon Inn	M40	12	166
General Tarleton	A1(M)	48	237
George & Dragon	A1(M)	8	216
George Hotel	M6	40	109
George IV	A1(M)	9	219
Globe Inn	M5	27	83
Green Dragon	M27	1	160
Green Man	M11	12	123
Greyhound	M6	39	105
Half Moon	M3	3	29
Hall Garth Hotel	A1(M)	59	244
Hardwick Hall Hotel	A1(M)	60	246
Hare & Hounds	M20	9	139
Hare & Hounds	M25	6	149
Harrow Inn	M2	5	23
Haywaggon	M6	1	89
Hazelwood Castle Hotel	A1(M)	45	231
Hit & Miss	M4	17	51
Hoghton Arms	M65	3	207
Hoole Hall Hotel	M53	12	182
Huntsman	M5	14	72
Jacksons Boat	M60	6	194
John Bull	M18	6	127
Jolly Huntsman	M4	17	50
Jubilee	M62	21	200
Kings Arms	M6	40	107
Kits Coty Restaurant	M20	6	134

INDEX *continued*

INDEX *continued*

INDEX *continued*

INDEX *continued*

SCOTLAND

INDEX BY MOTORWAYS AND JUNCTIONS

INDEX BY MOTORWAYS AND JUNCTIONS cont

INDEX BY MOTORWAYS AND JUNCTIONS *cont*

INDEX BY MOTORWAYS AND JUNCTIONS *cont*

INDEX BY MOTORWAYS
AND JUNCTIONS *cont*

READERS' RESPONSE

If you think that we have missed any places which should be included or that circumstances have altered, such as a change of ownership, which would mean an addition, amendment or even deletion, then please let us know using the following page(s).

If your suggestions are included in the next issue, we will send you a free copy of the new edition.

READERS RESPONSE

Name ....

Address..

....

....

.... Post Code. ....

T.N.................................... FAX...

E.Mail..

I would suggest that "A Break Off the Motorway" be amended as follows:

Inclusions

Name ....

Motorway.................... Junction.................... Location ....

Details ....

....

....

Amendments

Name. ....

Motorway.................... Junction.................... Location ....

Details ....

....

....

Deletions

Name ....

Motorway.................... Junction.................... Location ....

Details ....

....

....

Date........................... Signed...

READERS' RESPONSE

If you think that we have missed any places which should be included or that circumstances have altered, such as a change of ownership, which would mean an addition, amendment or even deletion, then please let us know using the following page(s).

If your suggestions are included in the next issue, we will send you a free copy of the new edition.

READERS RESPONSE

Name ....

Address...

....

....

.... Post Code. ....

T.N...................................... FAX ....

E.Mail...

I would suggest that "A Break Off the Motorway" be amended as follows:

Inclusions

Name ....

Motorway.................. Junction.................. Location ....

Details ....

....

....

Amendments

Name. ....

Motorway.................. Junction.................. Location ....

Details ....

....

....

Deletions

Name ....

Motorway.................. Junction.................. Location ....

Details ....

....

....

Date.......................... Signed...

READERS' RESPONSE

If you think that we have missed any places which should be included or that circumstances have altered, such as a change of ownership, which would mean an addition, amendment or even deletion, then please let us know using the following page(s).

If your suggestions are included in the next issue, we will send you a free copy of the new edition.

READERS RESPONSE

Name ....

Address..

....

....

.... Post Code. ....

T.N..................................... FAX ....

E.Mail..

I would suggest that "A Break Off the Motorway" be amended as follows:

Inclusions

Name ....

Motorway................... Junction................... Location ....

Details ....

....

....

Amendments

Name. ....

Motorway................... Junction................... Location ....

Details ....

....

....

Deletions

Name ....

Motorway................... Junction................... Location ....

Details ....

....

....

Date.......................... Signed..